"Given the contributors, I expected this book to be good, but it exceeds expectations. There's no weak link. Every chapter, including the introduction, brings a unique and vital perspective to a critical subject. It's impossible to overstate the power and eternal impact of our spoken and written words, for good or evil. With stylistic diversity but thematic unity, these men bring a rich, biblical, Christ-centered, interesting, and immensely helpful perspective. I wholeheartedly recommend it."

—RANDY ALCORN, author, *Heaven* and *If God Is Good*

"Solomon tells us, 'Death and life are in the power of the tongue, and those who love it will eat its fruits' (Prov. 18:21). Words kill and words give life; they're either poison or fruit. They have massive potential for both good and evil. They have the power to either build up or tear down. The contributors to this volume understand this well, and they show, in both theologically deep and practically down-to-earth ways, how the church must be marked by redemptive speech. They show how the sweetness and strength of the gospel—the sweetness of grace, the strength of truth—should flavor everything we say. John Piper asks, 'What would the world be like—the home, the church, the school, the public square—if words were used the way Jesus used them?' Read this book and find out."

—TULLIAN TCHIVIDJIAN, Pastor, Coral Ridge Presbyterian Church; author, *Unfashionable*

"A splendid book that deserves a spot on the bookshelf of every Christian communicator. Consider it a passport into the world of God-seeking, skilled wordsmiths. One insight after another—creative, practical, and drenched with wisdom."

—MAX LUCADO, author, *You Are Special* and the Wemmicks series

"Words are powerful. As the Scriptures indicate, they can create and destroy, build and burn down, save and condemn. The triune God created and upholds us by his Word, redeems us by renarrating our lives by his gospel, and directs us by his commands so that our words become more conformed to his Word. These many facets of verbal communication—both divine and human—are displayed in one rich and enriching jewel. Faith and practice are wonderfully integrated in this collection of godly wisdom."

—MICHAEL HORTON, J. G. Machen Professor of Systematic Theology and Apologetics, Westminster Seminary California

"In a culture dominated by the abundance of text messages, tweets, and status updates, we are in desperate need to have a biblical understanding of the power of words. Those who are serious about raising up the next generation of kingdom leaders will take heed to the Bible-saturated wisdom in this book and teach their staff and students to do the same. I know I will!"

—MATT BRADNER, Director, Campus Outreach, Lynchburg, Virginia

"Jesus Christ set the record straight when he declared that we do not live by bread alone but by every word that proceeds from the mouth of the Father. We live and die by words. Words are central to life, to communication, to meaning, and to Christian theology. This said, our relative inattentiveness to the meaning of words in the Christian church is to our shame. The contributors offer a rescue from this inattentiveness with wise words of spiritual counsel, deep words of doctrinal conviction, and saving words of the gospel. This book is urgently needed, and I am most pleased to recommend this volume with a good word."

    —R. ALBERT MOHLER JR., President, Southern Baptist
    Theological Seminary

"God's Word is not only the word he speaks to us; it is Jesus Christ himself, according to John 1:1–14. So God's speech is fundamental to who he is. Perhaps surprisingly for many of us, human life reflects God's word in this respect. Our words are central to our lives, as God's Word is to his. James 3:1–12 tells us that if we can control our tongues, we can control our whole lives. So we need to give a lot more thought to our language, its meaning and effects, and its relation to God's own Word. *The Power of Words and the Wonder of God* includes some scriptural, thoughtful essays on these subjects. I hope that it attracts many readers and much attention."

    —JOHN FRAME, Professor of Systematic Theology and Philosophy,
    Reformed Theological Seminary

"Read this book and you will be given a vision for your speech. You will speak less in some situations and more in others. You will be guided to speak both gently and with boldness. You will be more alert to what you say as you sing. You will say, 'Thank you, Lord, for words.' You will also say, 'Forgive me, Lord, for my casual and reckless words.' And—I thought this was a bonus— you will get to know the authors in a great Q&A."

    —EDWARD WELCH, Counselor and Faculty, Christian Counseling
    and Education Foundation

"This is a truly wonderful book on a timely and neglected subject. Our society is drowning in a glut of words and images; we do not need more of them. What we need is what this book can guide us to—the right kind of words used for the right ends. This collection of essays, consistently weighty in substance, makes good on the claims of the book's title: it convinces us of the power of words and instills a desire to see them used to express the wonder of God. My heart leaped many times as I read it."

    —LELAND RYKEN, Professor of English, Wheaton College

The Power of Words and
the Wonder of God

Other Books Coedited by
John Piper and Justin Taylor:

Stand: A Call for the Endurance of the Saints (2008)

The Supremacy of Christ in a Postmodern World (2007)

Suffering and the Sovereignty of God (2006)

Sex and the Supremacy of Christ (2005)

A God-Entranced Vision of All Things:
The Legacy of Jonathan Edwards (2004)

The Power of Words and the Wonder of God

John Piper and Justin Taylor
General Editors

:: CROSSWAY WHEATON, ILLINOIS

The Power of Words and the Wonder of God

Copyright © 2009 by Desiring God Ministries

Published by Crossway Books
    a publishing ministry of Good News Publishers
    1300 Crescent Street
    Wheaton, Illinois 60187

Cover design: Matthew Taylor, Taylor Design Works

First printing 2009

Printed in the United States of America

Trade paperback ISBN: 978-1-4335-1049-6

PDF ISBN: 978-1-4335-1050-2

Mobipocket ISBN: 978-1-4335-1051-9

ePub ISBN: 978-1-4335-2376-2

Library of Congress Cataloging-in-Publication Data
The power of words and the wonder of God / John Piper and
Justin Taylor, editors.
    p. cm.
    Includes indexes.
    ISBN 978-1-4335-1049-6 (tpb)
    1. Oral communication—Religious aspects—Christianity. I. Piper, John,
1946–   . II. Taylor, Justin, 1976–   . III. Title.
BV4597.53.C64P69   2009
241'.672—dc22   2009010899

MLY		18	17	16	15	14	13	12	11	10	09
14	13	12	11	10	9	8	7	6	5	4	3	2	1

In Memory of
John Bunyan

Of whose great *Pilgrim* book he truly wrote:

This book is writ in such a dialect
As may the minds of listless men affect:
It seems a novelty, and yet contains
Nothing but sound and honest gospel strains.

Contents

Contributors   11

Acknowledgments   13

Introduction   15
Justin Taylor

1   War of Words: Getting to the Heart for God's Sake   23
Paul David Tripp

2   The Bit, the Bridle, and the Blessing: An Exposition of James 3:1–12   45
Sinclair B. Ferguson

3   Is There Christian Eloquence? Clear Words and the Wonder of the Cross   67
John Piper

4   How Sharp the Edge? Christ, Controversy, and Cutting Words   81
Mark Driscoll

5   Story-shaped Faith   105
Daniel Taylor

6   Words of Wonder: What Happens When We Sing?   121
Bob Kauflin

Part 1: A Conversation with the Contributors   137
John Piper, Mark Driscoll, Sinclair Ferguson, and Justin Taylor

Part 2: A Conversation with the Contributors   149
John Piper, Bob Kauflin, Paul Tripp, Daniel Taylor, and Justin Taylor

Notes   162

Subject Index   167

Scripture Index   171

Desiring God: Note on Resources   175

Contributors

Mark Driscoll is a founding pastor and the lead preaching pastor of Mars Hill Church in Seattle. He is president of the Acts 29 Church Planting Network (www.acts29network.org) and leads the Resurgence Missional Theology Cooperative (www.theresurgence.com). His books include *Vintage Jesus*; *Death by Love*; *Vintage Church*; and *Religion Saves*. Mark and his wife, Grace, have five children.

Sinclair B. Ferguson is the senior minister of the First Presbyterian Church in Columbia, South Carolina, and professor of systematic theology at Redeemer Seminary in Dallas. He is the author of several books, the most recent being *In Christ Alone: Reflections on the Heart of the Gospel*, and *Westminster Directory of Public Worship* (co-authored with Mark Dever). Sinclair and his wife, Dorothy, have four grown children.

Bob Kauflin is the director of worship development for Sovereign Grace Ministries in Gaithersburg, Maryland. After receiving a piano performance degree from Temple University in 1976, he traveled for eight years with the contemporary Christian group GLAD as a songwriter, speaker, and arranger. His current role involves equipping pastors and musicians in the theology and practice of congregational worship, contributing to Sovereign Grace recordings, and being one of the worship leaders at Covenant Life Church, where he has served since 1997. His first book, *Worship Matters: Leading Others to Encounter the Greatness of God,* was published in 2008 by Crossway, and his blog is titled the same (www.worshipmatters.com). Bob and his wife, Julie, have six children and seven grandchildren.

John Piper is the pastor for preaching at Bethlehem Baptist Church in Minneapolis, Minnesota, where he has served since 1980 seeking to "spread a passion for the supremacy of God in all things for the joy of all peoples through Jesus Christ." John has written over forty books, including *Desiring God*; *Don't Waste Your Life*; *Fifty Reasons Why Jesus Came to Die*; *What Jesus Demands from the World*; *When I Don't Desire God*; and *God Is the Gospel*. John and his wife, Noël, have five children and a growing number of grandchildren.

Daniel Taylor is a professor of literature and writing at Bethel University in Saint Paul, Minnesota, where he has taught since 1977. He speaks internationally on issues related to story, values, character, faith, and contemporary culture. Among his books are *Tell Me a Story: The Life-Shaping Power of Our Stories*; *Letters to My Children: A Father Passes on His Values*; and most recently, *In Search of Sacred Places: Looking for Wisdom on Celtic Holy Islands*. Taylor is also the cofounder of The Legacy Center (www.thelegacycenter. net), which encourages people and organizations to identify and preserve the values and stories that have shaped their lives. Dan and his wife, Jayne, have four children and two granddaughters.

Justin Taylor is editorial director at Crossway Books in Wheaton, Illinois. Prior to this position he served as director of theological research and education at Desiring God Ministries. With John Piper he edited five previous conference books, and coedited with Kelly Kapic two new editions of works by John Owen. He blogs daily at Between Two Worlds. Justin and his wife, Lea, have three young children.

Paul David Tripp has an extensive speaking ministry, both nationally and internationally, as president of Paul Tripp Ministries (www. paultrippministries.org). He is also on the pastoral staff at Tenth Presbyterian Church in Philadelphia, where he preaches on Sunday evenings and leads the Ministry to Center City. He is the author of numerous books. Most notably related to the theme of the present volume is his book *War of Words: Getting to the Heart of Our Communication Struggles*. Recently he has written *A Quest for More*; *Whiter Than Snow*; and *A Shelter in the Time of Storm*. Paul and his wife, Luella, have four grown children.

Acknowledgments

Our editor, Lydia Brownback, and indexers, David Mathis and Carol Steinbach, have helped us once again to make this book better and more useful. Thank you for serving us, and for serving readers of this book.

At Desiring God, we give thanks to God for Jon Bloom, the executive director; Scott Anderson, who oversaw the conference where these chapters were originally presented; and David Mathis, who serves John with diligence and care.

We are also thankful to the leadership at Crossway Books—especially Lane Dennis and Allan Fisher—who agreed to publish this book and who share our vision for God-centered materials that build up the body of Christ.

Most importantly, we thank God for the gift of his Son Jesus Christ. We say with the apostle Peter, "Lord, to whom shall we go? You have the words of eternal life" (John 6:68).

Introduction

Justin Taylor

WORDS. We think words, hear words, speak words, sing words, write words, and read words—all the time. Every day.

What do words have to do with Christianity? Almost everything. At every stage in redemptive history—from the time before time, to God's creation, to man's fall, to Christ's redemption, and to the coming consummation—"God is there and he is not silent."[1] God's words decisively create, confront, convict, correct, and comfort. By his words he both interprets and instructs.

The Opening Scenes of the Bible

If you wanted to construct a biblical theology of words, you could get pretty far in just the first few pages of your Bible. The early chapters of Genesis are replete with God using words to create and order, name and interpret, bless and curse, instruct and warn.

God *speaks* ("And God said, 'Let there be . . . '"), and reality results ("and there was. . . ." "And it was so"). He *names* ("God called . . . "), and things are publicly identified. We learn later that it is "by the word of his power" that God's Son, Jesus Christ, continually *sustains* and "upholds the universe" (Heb. 1:3).

Before God creates man, he first uses words to announce his intention ("Let us make . . . "). And once Adam and Eve are created, their first experience with God involves words, as he gives them the cultural mandate (Be fruitful, multiply, fill the earth, subdue it, have dominion), explains their freedom ("You may . . . "), and warns them against disobeying his command ("You shall not . . . ").

When Satan slithers onto the scene as a crafty serpent, his first action is to speak, and his wicked words are designed to call into question the very words of God. The first step is to sow the seed of doubt ("Did God *actually* say . . . ?"). And the second step is the explicit accusation that the Creator was really a liar ("You will not surely die").

When Adam and Eve rebel against the only restriction they were given, they express for the first time words that are so common for us today: fear ("I was afraid"), shame ("I hid myself"), and blame (that woman—whom *you* gave to be with me!).

God then interprets their new fallen world for them—and also gives the first words of the gospel, foretelling the time when he will send his Son to save his people and crush the head of his enemy. God uses words to tell of the coming Word made flesh (John 1).

Jesus, the Word Made Flesh

When God's Son eventually enters into human history as the God-man, he lives by God's Word (Luke 4:4), keeps God's Word (John 8:55), and preaches God's Word (Mark 2:2). The Father gave Jesus words, Jesus gave them to his followers, and his followers received them (John 17:8).

Jesus' words are inseparable from his person[2] and thus can be identified as having divine attributes. To be ashamed of Christ's words is on the same level as being ashamed of Christ himself (Luke 9:26). His words are eternal: unlike heaven and earth, Christ's words will remain forever (Matt. 24:35). They have power: Jesus could cast out spirits with "a word" (Matt. 8:16); he merely had to "say the word" and someone could be healed (Matt. 8:8). Jesus' words are "spirit and life," "the words of eternal life" (John 6:63, 68). Jesus' words dwell or abide in those who are united to Christ and abiding in him (John 8:31; John 15:7; Col. 3:16). Only those who hear and keep Jesus' word receive blessing and eternal life (Luke 11:28; John 5:24; 8:47, 52).

Those who heard him were "amazed at his words" (Mark 10:24), hanging on every word and marveling at his gracious speech (Luke 19:48; 4:22). They recognized that his words possessed a unique authority (Luke 4:32).

But Jesus critiqued those who used the words of their prayers to conceal the hypocrisy of their hearts, heaping up "empty phrases" and wanting to be "heard for their many words" (Matt.

6:7). He accused them of using their traditions to make "void the word of God" (Matt. 15:6). His own words found no place in their hearts—some couldn't bear to hear his words, and some heard his words but refused to keep them (John 8:37, 43; 14:24). In response, Jesus' enemies "plotted how to entangle him in his talk" (Matt. 22:15).

Jesus warned that how one hears and responds to Jesus' words reveals the ultimate dividing line within salvation history: on the day of judgment we will each give an account "for every careless word," being either justified or condemned by our words (Matt. 12:36–37), for "what comes out of the mouth proceeds from the heart" (Matt. 15:18). If you hear and practice Christ's words, you are like a wise man building a house on a rock-solid foundation that can remain standing even during a torrential storm. But hearing Christ's words and failing to do them is like building a house on sand, which will crumble to the ground in the midst of the storm (Matt. 7:24–26).

Words and the Gospel

In the book of Acts and in the Epistles, the gospel message—the good and glorious news that "another true and obedient human being has come on our behalf, that he has lived for us the kind of life we should live but can't, that he has paid fully the penalty we deserve for the life we do live but shouldn't,"[3] with all of the personal and kingdom implications that that entails—is referred to as "the Word."

As you read God's Word and consider the deep implications of the gospel for your life, you'll begin to discern a pattern: (1) God has holy standards for how we are to speak words and listen to words. (2) This side of heaven we will never fully measure up to God's holy standard regarding the use of our tongue. (3) Jesus fulfilled what we (along with Adam, Israel, and every prophet, priest, and king) failed to do: his words were perfect words, without sin. By his punishment-bearing, substitutionary death, his words can become our words. (4) Our day-by-day failure to use our tongue as we ought—for God's glory and for the good of his people—comes from a functional rejection of Christ the Word. It is only as we look to Jesus, rejoicing in him and in his atoning provision, that we are freed to walk—and talk—in his way.[4]

How Should We Then Live?

If God is a God of words, and if Jesus and his gospel are inseparable, then how should we—those who seek to follow him—use our words?

The book of Proverbs is an excellent place to start, giving pithy statements about what godly and ungodly speech looks like. For a sampling, consider these contrasts:

PROVERB	GODLY WORDS	UNGODLY WORDS
10:32	The *lips* of the righteous know what is acceptable.	The *mouth* of the wicked [knows] what is perverse.
12:18	The *tongue* of the wise brings healing.	Rash *words* are like sword thrusts.
13:1	A wise son *hears* his father's instruction.	A *scoffer* does not *listen* to rebuke.
13:3	Whoever guards his *mouth* preserves his life.	He who opens wide his *lips* comes to ruin.
13:10	With those who *take advice* is wisdom.	By *insolence* comes nothing but strife.
13:18	Whoever *heeds reproof* is honored.	Poverty and disgrace come to him who *ignores instruction*.
14:3	The *lips* of the wise will preserve them.	By the *mouth* of a fool comes a rod for his back.
14:25	A *truthful witness* saves lives.	One who *breathes out lies* is deceitful.
15:1	A *soft answer* turns away wrath.	A *harsh word* stirs up anger.

But there is so much more that can and should be said. In the pages of this book you'll find six authors who are striving to help us understand God's perspective on words. Whether it's the words of relationships, words of eloquence, words of sarcasm, words of story, or words of song—all of these have to do with who we are and how we speak. What follows is an attempt to summarize briefly their chapters.

Paul Tripp

Tripp explains what all of us already know: our world of talk is a world of trouble. But in order to understand the war of words, we must first understand the war for the heart. Word problems are heart problems. Within each of our hearts there is a war between two kingdoms—the kingdom of self and the kingdom of God. One of the two is always ruling our hearts and shaping our talk. And only when our hearts are ruled by love—marked by self sacrifice for the redemptive good of others no matter what—will we overflow with wholesome words of love and grace.

Sinclair Ferguson

Ferguson expounds James 3:1–12, identifying four driving principles regarding the tongue: (1) the tongue is difficult to *tame*; (2) the tongue has a disproportionate *power*; (3) the tongue causes *destruction*; and (4) the tongue is plagued with a deadly *inconsistency*. After unpacking this imagery and showing the gospel implications, Ferguson exhorts us: (1) to realize that the depth of our sin, the pollution of our hearts, and our need of saving grace are all evidenced in our use of the tongue; (2) to recognize we are each a new creation in Christ; and (3) to continue in the Word.

John Piper

Eloquence involves combining words in order to make an impact on the listener or the reader. The apostle Paul said that he was sent by Christ to preach the gospel, but not to preach it with "eloquent wisdom" or with "lofty speech" (1 Cor. 1:17; 2:1). In fact, Paul, says, using such eloquence would empty the cross of its power. Piper, through a study of 1 Corinthians, explores whether this means that eloquence—which the Bible itself seems to exhibit!—is discouraged. Piper concludes that Paul is discouraging a certain form of eloquence that is motivated by the exploitation of self and the belittling or ignoring of God. Biblically sanctioned eloquence, he argues, should humbly exalt Christ with the hope that God will use our language to help listeners retain interest, increase sympathy, awaken sensitivity, and feel the words powerfully.

Mark Driscoll

Driscoll argues that Scripture specifies four functions of the way in which shepherds should relate to those inside and outside the church. They are to *feed the sheep* (Christians, the flock of Jesus the Good Shepherd); *rebuke the swine* (who claim to worship God but live unrepentant lives in filthy sin); *shoot the wolves* (heretics, false teachers, and anyone who ravages the flock and feasts on the sheep); and *beat the dogs* (who bark at God's people in an effort to control, intimidate, manipulate, use, abuse, terrify, harm, and devour them). The people in the undershepherd's flock, in return, should *pray for their pastor-shepherds*, that God would give them a discerning mind, thick skin, a good sense of humor, a tender heart, a humble disposition, a supportive family, and evangelistic devotion.

Daniel Taylor

Taylor (related to me only in Christ!) argues that the best way to conceive of the Christian faith, and the faithful life, is to see yourself as a character in the greatest story ever told—a story to be lived, and not merely a set of propositions to be believed. The Bible, in other words, tells a master story and invites us to make it our personal story. Because all good stories are centered on characters making difficult choices with uncertain outcomes, we need to understand how the story of faith necessarily shapes how we live. Taylor illustrates all of this with a few stories of his own, showing that stories come from God and need to be passed on to the next generation.

Bob Kauflin

Kauflin argues that Christians tend to fall into one of three categories when it comes to the relationship between music and words: (1) music *supersedes* the word; (2) music *undermines* the word; (3) music *serves* the word. Arguing for this third paradigm, Kauflin suggests three implications: (1) *Singing can help us remember words*, which means that we should use melodies that are effective, sing words that God wants us to remember, and seek to memorize songs. (2) *Singing can help us engage emotionally with words*, which means that we need a broader emotional range in the songs we sing, and that singing them should be an emotional event. (3) *Singing can help us use words to demonstrate and express our unity*, which means singing songs that unite us instead of divide us, recognizing that musical creativity in the church has functional limits and that it is ultimately the gospel, not music, that unites us in Christ.

Our Prayer

When Moses stood before the Israelites, he spoke to them the words of a prayer-song, which began like this:

> Give ear, O heavens, and I will speak,
>   and let the earth hear the words of my mouth.
> May my teaching drop as the rain,
>   my speech distill as the dew,
> like gentle rain upon the tender grass,
>   and like showers upon the herb.
> For I will proclaim the name of the Lord;
>   ascribe greatness to our God! (Deut. 32:1–3)

This is our prayer for this book as well. May our great and glorious God graciously use these imperfect words to equip and encourage you in a path of using life-giving words to honor his name, edify the church, and call the lost to the gospel of Jesus Christ.

CHAPTER ONE

War of Words: Getting to the Heart for God's Sake

Paul David Tripp

I DON'T KNOW VERY MANY OF YOU, but there are three things that I know about you.

Three Things I Know about You

1) You Talk

First, I know you talk. Oh, my goodness, do you talk. Some of us more than others—some of us have trouble stopping—but all of us talk every day. Yes, even though we aren't always aware of it, every day of our lives is filled with talk. Every moment is infected with talk. Every relationship and situation is dyed with words. We're word-ish people. You could hardly identify a more formative aspect of our daily lives than our world of words. Yet whenever I begin to think, speak, or write about this topic, I experience a bit of frustration. What frustrates me is the vocabulary of communication. The terms are so mundane—*words, talk, dialogue, conversation, communication.* They just don't seem to carry the freight of how profoundly significant and important this area of life actually is.

Think with me about the significance of this part of our lives. We have to start by acknowledging that the very first words ever spoken were not spoken by a human being. The very first words ever spoken were spoken by God. Perhaps one of the ways that

I'm most obviously God-like is that like God, I talk. You and I will never understand the profound importance of words unless we start here. Words belong to the Lord. What this means is that whenever you take words as belonging to you, your words lose their shelter from difficulty. You have never spoken a word that belongs to you, because words belong to the Lord. We think that words are not that important because we think of words as little utilitarian tools for making our life easier and more efficient, when they are actually a powerful gift given by a communicating God for his divine purpose.

All of us are tricked into thinking that words aren't really that important, because they fill all those little mundane moments of our lives. Maybe that's exactly why they are profoundly important. I don't want to hurt your feelings, but you only make three or four big decisions in your life. Most of us won't be written up in history books. Several decades after you die, the people you leave behind will struggle to remember the events of your life. You live your life in the utterly mundane. And if God doesn't rule your mundane, he doesn't rule you, because that's where you live.

The book of Proverbs is, in ways, a treatise on talk. I would summarize it this way: *words give life; words bring death—you choose.* What does this mean? It means you have never spoken a neutral word in your life. Your words have direction to them. If your words are moving in the *life* direction, they will be words of encouragement, hope, love, peace, unity, instruction, wisdom, and correction. But if your words are moving in a *death* direction, they will be words of anger, malice, slander, jealousy, gossip, division, contempt, racism, violence, judgment, and condemnation. Your words have direction to them. When you hear the word *talk* you ought to hear something that is high and holy and significant and important. May God help us never to look at talk as something that doesn't matter.

2) The Saddest and Most Celebratory Moments of Your Life Have Been Accompanied by Talk

There's a second thing I know about you. I know that the saddest and most celebratory moments of your life have been accompanied by talk. When I stand up to speak or sit down to write, I feel like there's a company of a hundred people behind me who have all contributed to everything I know, everything I speak, and everything I think about the ways of my Lord. These people have written and spoken into my ears glorious and celebratory truths that have penetrated my heart and changed everything in my life. I'll celebrate God's gift of the words of these people forever.

I also have sat with people who are thirty-five, forty-five, or fifty years old who'll talk to me about horrible things that their mom and dad said to them decades ago. When they begin to recount the ugly words of yesteryear, they'll weep as if it happened yesterday. In these moments, I'm confronted again with the scary, painful, long-term shelf life of ugly, hateful, abusive talk.

On the other hand, what's more exciting than waiting for a child to speak his or her first words? Little Jimmy toddles into the room and he goes *blu-blah-blah-blah*. And Dad says to his wife, "I think he said 'John Calvin.' I'm sure. I'm sure it was 'John Calvin.'" Well, it was probably just gas, but the parents are expectant and excited because Jimmy is on the cusp of something that is magnificently human—he is getting ready to talk!

What is sadder in all of life than when a human being goes silent? I remember it well with my dear mom. We actually had some preparation. She had been sick for a while, and we were called to her bedside. We knew that this was the end, but we were privileged to spend her final week with her. We sang to Mom every hymn in Christendom. I finally bent over her bed and whispered in her ear, "Mom, we're out of hymns, we're going to sing to you the Beatles." She smiled. But with all that preparation I was not ready for that moment when Mom fell silent. There was something horrible and de-human about that moment. I wanted to hear her say "I love you" one more time. I wanted to finish conversations that we had never finished. I had so much that I wanted to say, so much that I wanted to hear. But she had spoken her last words.

You see, talk is a very, very important dimension of your humanity, your God-likeness. So your saddest and most celebratory moments of life have all been accompanied by talk.

3) Your World of Talk Is a World of Trouble

There's a third thing that I know about everyone reading this book: your world of talk is a world of trouble. I know this for sure, not because I know you but because I know me. It's to my grief that I am not writing these words as an expert. No, I'm writing as a man in moment-by-moment need of the rescuing grace of my Redeemer. And you are reading these words as a person in the same kind of need. Who of you would be quite comfortable if I were to play a public recording of everything you said last month? I don't think any of you would volunteer.

My wife, Luella, and I have been married for thirty-seven years. During those thirty-seven years, Luella and I have had a particular struggle in our marriage. Well, it's really my struggle. It's over the issue of time. Luella was raised in Cuba, and she has a combination of a sort of island view of time and a Latin view of time. She lives on a bit of a vibe. People go to the islands because time slows down. On the other hand, I was raised by a man who thought that the sole litmus test of the value of a human being was punctuality. If you're on time, you can live. It's an understatement to say that being on time is a bit of a struggle.

Let me illustrate for you. Once, when our children were young, we decided to go to a state park for a picnic, and we agreed we would leave at three o'clock. For me, a time set the law of the Medes and Persians that cannot be broken. For Luella, it's a rough estimate. At about 3:15 I realized that we wouldn't be leaving on time, and I began to get upset. And Luella informed me of something radical: we didn't, in fact, have an appointment at the park. No one was going to remove our table and suck the water out of the lake and roll back the grass and remove the trees. It was okay if we arrived a little later.

Well, all of that background is to help you understand the particular situation I am about to share with you. It was Easter morning in the Tripp family. I think that those of you with children can relate to this; Sunday morning isn't often the most relaxed time of the week. We stuff children in vans saying, "Shut up. We're going to worship." But this was not just another Sunday; this was Easter morning, and our church, for reasons I don't really understand, had decided that one of the best ways to celebrate the resurrection was to have a full breakfast before the service, which meant that we had to wake and leave about an hour and a half earlier than the usual Sunday time. I woke up with feelings of utter futility.

About forty-five minutes later, I walked into the bathroom where Luella was, along with my then nine-year-old son, and I could tell by the way she was dressed that she was not near being ready. So I began to say helpful things to her, like informing her that it was not an Easter *dinner*; it was an Easter *breakfast*. She found that very helpful. I told her that a couple of our children were already in the car, as usual, waiting. I reminded her that I was an elder in the church and my arrival before the ham and eggs was very important to my ministry.

About then my nine-year-old son said, "Daddy, may I say something?" I should have said no. I said, "Sure, you can talk." He said, "Daddy, do you really think this is the way a Christian man should be talking to his wife?" Now, I'm a counselor sort of person. I'm pretty good at these conversations, so I said, "What do you think?" trying to escape the conviction. And little Darnay, not trying to be impertinent, said out of his little heart of faith, "Daddy, it doesn't make any difference what I think. What does God think?" I slogged out of the bathroom being duly chided, and as I got to the threshold of the door, I heard his little voice say to me, "May I say something else?" I wanted to say, "No, no, please don't!" He said, "What I mean, Dad, is what does the Bible say about it?"

I went to my bedroom and was hit immediately with a couple of thoughts. First my pride reared up. I wanted to be a hero to my son. I was embarrassed that he had seen through my harsh communication, and he had hurt for his mommy. But that thought didn't last very long. I was filled with the wonder of his question. How could it be that God would love me this much that he would give a twit of care about that mundane little incidental moment in the Tripp family? This is just one moment in one morning of one day of one week of one month of one year of one family living on one street in one neighborhood in one city in one state in one nation in one hemisphere in the globe in one moment of time. And God, in the glory of his love, was in that moment. God cares for me so much that he would raise up a nine-year-old boy to rescue my heart one more time. That is love so magnificent I can't wrap my brain around it.

You see, that love, that redeeming love is not just a big-moment love. That love reaches into the private recesses of your everyday life. It reaches into those secret, quiet moments, even into seemingly trivial moments in a bathroom on a single day. That's how zealous that redeeming love actually is, and because of that I can have—you can have, we can have—the courage to look at this difficult area of our talk. The gospel is so robust we don't need to be afraid of looking at the horror of the trouble of our world of talk, because Jesus *is*—and because he's our *Savior.*

So What's the Struggle with Our Talk Anyway?

In this chapter I want to take you on a bit of a biblical tour, and I want to ask, What is the trouble with our talk? What is the difficulty? Why is it that all of us get into talk trouble? Why do all of us look back and wish there were words we had never said? We all have had conversations we wish we could snatch out of history. We wish we could remove them from the memory of the people that heard them. I wish I could say that I'm proud of everything I've said to my children and to Luella, but I cannot say that. We simply have to ask, "What is that trouble with our words?"

Before we answer, I want to make a comment on the Bible that will provide the basis for our answer. I don't know if you've noticed this, but your Bible isn't arranged by topic. Some of you are irritated by that. You wish it was chopped up into topics, and if there were topical tabs on the side of your Bible, that would make it even easier. The Bible isn't arranged that way, but not because of accident or oversight. It's arranged that way because it was God's intention to give us his book in the form that we have it. The Bible is essentially a story. It's the grand narrative of redemption. It is actually more accurate to say that the Bible is a theologically annotated story. It's a story with God's notes. There are *propositions* alongside the story that are truth statements that help you to understand the plot of God's story. Also alongside the story are *principles* that apply the story to your life so you can live inside of the plot of God's story. God has given his Word in this way because his call to us is that we would live with a "God's story mentality." This means that in the situations and relationships where God has placed us, we are to live in a way that is consistent with the plot of God's story. God's Word is not just given to be informational but transformational of the way we live.

If all you do is run to the obvious communication passages in

Scripture, you miss most of what the Bible has to say about your world of talk because to the degree that every passage opens up to you the nature of God, of his grace, of your sin, of life in a fallen world, and the nature of the processes of redemption—to that degree every passage gives you information that helps you to understand this world of talk.

Let's look at the first passage that will help us understand our struggle with words. There is no better place to begin than with Luke 6:43–45:

> For no good tree bears bad fruit, nor again does a bad tree bear good fruit, for each tree is known by its own fruit. For figs are not gathered from thornbushes, nor are grapes picked from a bramble bush. The good person out of the good treasure of his heart produces good, and the evil person out of his evil treasure produces evil, for out of the abundance of the heart his mouth speaks.

Christ is saying something significant and important. It challenges a very tempting perspective that all of us struggle with. Christ is teaching us that we live out of our hearts.

Let's think about the language here. What does the Bible mean when it uses that word *heart*? The Bible essentially divides you into two pieces—your outer man and your inner man. The outer man is your physical self. It's the house God has given you for your heart while you are here on earth. You could call your body your earth suit. The Bible uses many words for the inner man: mind, emotion, soul, spirit, will. These words are all summarized by a big-basket term—*heart*. This term is used in almost a thousand passages of Scripture. It's one of the most well-developed themes in all of the Bible. When the Bible uses the term *heart*, it means the *causal core of your personhood*. The heart is your directional system. The heart is your steering wheel. Your behavior isn't caused by the situations and relationships outside of you. This passage teaches that your experiences *influence*, but do not *determine*, your behavior. Your behavior is shaped and caused by how your heart reacts to and interacts with the situations and relationships that are outside of you.

Jesus uses a wonderful example in the Luke passage. He says it is "out of the abundance of the heart his mouth speaks" (v. 45). Let this sink in for a moment. I am convinced that you and I don't want to believe that. Have you ever said to someone, "Oh, I didn't mean to say that"? It would be more biblical to say, "Please, forgive me for saying what I meant," because if it hadn't first been in your heart, it wouldn't have come out of your mouth.

My mom was a member of a Depression-era family of ten brothers and sisters. Her family was what our culture would call a classic dysfunctional family. They didn't like one another very much, but they were committed to family reunions! They were creepy sort of gatherings, I must admit. The family would gather in a hall, and as they arrived they would sit like warring nation states, sort of like a bad U.N.—or maybe like the real U.N.!

The centerpiece of the day would be a huge potluck. Everybody would bring their best dish. After the meal enough alcohol would come out to float the United States, and the family gathering would get very wild. My parents got into the habit of leaving just after the meal. They taught us how to work the table and say hello to our aunts and uncles and cousins, and before the thing got too crazy, we beat our retreat.

During one of these gatherings, my mom got involved in an evangelistic encounter with one of her siblings and didn't realize that one of her brothers had gotten very drunk. My uncle was in the room where my brother Mark and I were, and he was saying sexually perverse things about the women. My mom realized that was happening, and she ran downstairs and grabbed Mark and me and yanked us to the car. I remember it very well; I don't think our feet touched the steps. She stuffed us in the car, and before she drove away she said, "Paul and Mark, I want to say something to you, and I want you never to forget it." What she said was actually an eloquent summary of this passage in Luke. She said, "There's nothing that comes out of the mouth of a drunk that wasn't there in the first place."

The alcohol didn't create the sexual perversion that came out of my uncle's mouth. He was actually thinking those thoughts in his sobriety. What did the alcohol do? It loosened the lips, and when his lips got loose, out came the heart. Here is what you and I need to understand: *word problems are heart problems*. Word problems are not vocabulary problems. Word problems are not technique problems. Word problems in their essential form are heart problems.

Christ uses a wonderful example to drive this reality home. It's the example of a tree. What's the best way to recognize an apple tree? Well, it's obvious—apples. But when you look at those apples, you instinctively know that the tree you're looking at is apple-istic all the way down to its roots. If there wasn't apple-ism in its roots, it wouldn't grow apples as fruit. You will never, ever plant peach pits and get apples. Now, don't miss the profound point that Christ is making here. He is teaching the principle of organic consistency. There is an organic consistency between what's in our hearts and what comes out of our mouths.

The Essential Confession

I don't know about you, but I don't want to believe that. I actually want to believe that when it comes to communication, my biggest problem is outside of me, not inside of me. I want to think that it's my kids, my wife, my neighbors, my boss. I want to think that my greatest, deepest communication problem doesn't exist inside of me; it exists outside of me. But that, brothers and sisters, is a very dangerous heresy, because when you are able to convince yourself that your deepest, greatest problems in life exist outside of you, you'll quit being a seeker after the transforming grace of the Lord Jesus Christ. But we all ease our consciences with this heresy, telling ourselves that we said what we said only because of what someone said or did to us. We tell ourselves that our problem is not us, but them. My mom captured this response very well for me. She said, "Paul, I know that Scripture says, 'A soft answer turns away wrath and a harsh word stirs up anger,' but the person who wrote that didn't have my children."

Are you prepared to make this essential confession with me: "I am my greatest communication problem. The greatest difficulty, the greatest danger, and the everyday traps of communication that we all fall into all exist inside of me, not outside of me."

Let's go back to the tree. Pretend with me that I have an apple tree in my backyard in Philadelphia, and every year it grows dry, pulpy, brown, hard, and inedible apples, and it drives Luella crazy. So she says, "Paul, why would we have this apple tree if we can never eat these apples?"

I think and I ponder. I want to help this lady that I love. So after some contemplation I say to her, "I've come up with an idea. I think I can fix our apple tree."

She's a bit confused, but she's excited. Saturday morning she looks out the window and sees me carrying some items. Pay careful attention: I'm carrying a big, tall ladder, some branch cutters, an industrial grade pneumatic nail gun, and three bushels of Red Delicious apples. She watches me climb up on that ladder and very carefully cut off all those inedible apples. I nail Red Delicious apples carefully and symmetrically all around the tree. From a hundred yards away you would think I was the horticulturalist of the century. But what are you thinking if you're my wife? You're thinking, "This is the big one. The doctor said he'd be this way if he lived."

What's going to happen to those apples? They are going to rot, because they are not attached to the life-giving resources of the tree. More importantly, what kind of apples is that tree going to grow the next year? Twisted, pulpy, dried, brown, inedible apples, because there has been no organic change in that tree. If that tree is producing that kind of apple year after year, there is something systemically wrong with the tree, even down to its roots.

Let me apply this powerful physical picture to our world of talk. I am convinced that much of what we do in an attempt to change our communication is nothing more or less than apple nailing. It has no energy to understand and confess the war for the heart that lies beneath the war of words. People aren't my problem. Situations are not my problem. Circumstances are not my problem. Locations are not my problem. My problem is in my heart. It's only when you and I stand before our Redeemer and are humbly willing to say, regardless of the flawed people that you live with and the fallen world that is your address, that you are your greatest communication problem, that you are heading in a direction of fundamental biblical change in your world of talk.

Understanding the War of Words Means Understanding the War for the Heart

What is that war for the heart? I think it is most briefly and clearly summarized in a little phrase in 2 Corinthians 5:15. Here Paul is giving a bit of an explanation and a defense of his ministry, and he says one of those brief little phrases that's like opening a door to a universe of explanation and understanding: "Jesus died so that those who live would no longer live for themselves." Sin does something terrible to me. Sin turns me in on myself. Sin shrinks my life to the size of my life. Sin makes me obsessed with my wants, my needs, my feelings. Think about this, brothers and sisters. Sin is fundamentally antisocial, because sin causes me to love me more than anything else and to care for me more than anything else. It causes me to be obsessed by what I want, how I want it, when I want it, why I want it, where I want it, and whom I want to deliver it. Sin makes my life little more than "I want, I want, I want, I want, I want, I want, I want, I want, I want, I want, I want, I want, I want, I want, I want, I want, I want, I want, I want, I want (are you getting the point?), I want. Sin morphs all of us into a bottomless vat of demands. I'm a vat of expectancy. I'm a vat of entitlement. I wish I could say that this is not the true me, but it is.

Why am I irritated when I'm in traffic? I am irritated because I want to drive on roads paid for by other citizens who choose not to use them. Why am I irritated when my children mess up? I am irritated because I want self-parenting children. I want children who would say to me at every moment of parental instruction, "Yes, Dad. Of course, Dad. You're my father, O wise one that you are." I want my wife to say, "Of course, dear, you're right. You're always right. I have enjoyed so much living in the glory of your rightness." I want chocolate at ready reach. Sadly, my life is often reduced to, "I want, I want, I want." I am so full of a self-focused, self-oriented agenda that you can't even serve me.

I have an eye condition. I don't see very well at night because my eyes don't shift well between the light and the darkness, and it makes driving a little bit dangerous. I've told Luella that I have figured out how to handle it: there are mobile blobs and stationary blobs, and when I'm driving, the idea is to avoid them both. That doesn't make Luella very secure, so she has offered to do the driving for us. She does that because she loves me. She doesn't mind serving me in that way. That's a blessing. I don't deserve the love or service of anyone.

On one occasion we headed out toward an agreed-upon location, and we got to a place where I would have turned but she went straight. I couldn't leave that alone. I said, "Why didn't you turn?"

She said, "This is the way that I go."

I couldn't leave that alone. I said, "I think it's the wrong way."

She said something very logical: "Paul, I don't think it's a matter of right and wrong. I just think it's a matter of preference."

I couldn't leave that alone. I said, "What if my preference is right? You know, Luella, the shortest distance between two points is a straight line."

She said, "That's why I didn't turn." She added, "You know, Paul, why don't we do this—when you drive, you choose the direction, and when I drive, I'll choose the direction."

That seems logical, right? I couldn't leave that alone. I said to her, "Luella, if we were in a helicopter right now, flying over the city of Philadelphia, and we were to swoop down on this moment, you would know that my way is the right way."

Luella looked at me very seriously and said, "Paul Tripp, I don't think a helicopter is what you need right now."

I want. I want. I want. I want. I want. I want. I want. I tend to live in the claustrophobic confines of my own little self-defined world. I was not designed to live that way. I was created to live in the big-sky country of the glory of the kingdom of God with expansive borders beyond anything I could imagine or want for myself. My life was structured to be directed not so much by my desire for me but by the desires of Another for me. But I not only want to live in my little kingdom, I also want to co-opt the people around me into service of my kingdom.

I don't think I'm alone. Let me take you to an all-too-typical family scene. It's 10:30 at night and the children you put to bed at 9:00 are now fighting in their beds. You start down the hallway, feet heavy on the floorboards. You're probably not saying, "Thank you, Jesus, for this wonderful opportunity, part of the work of your kingdom. I so love redemption. I love this opportunity to be part of what you're doing." Instead you're probably saying, "They're dead!" And you burst into your children's room and say, "Do you know what my day's been like? Do you have any idea what I do? I don't ask for much—just children who are from earth. Why, I bought every shred of clothes you put on that back of yours. I bought every morsel of food you put in that big mouth of yours. I made your Christmases happy."

As you are ranting, do you think that your children are saying, "My, this is helpful . . . here is a person of distinct wisdom . . . I am so glad he came into my room . . . I think I'm seeing my heart"? No, your children gain little from the encounter and can't wait until you get out of their room.

Let's examine the emotion that is propelling you at the moment. You're not angry because your children have broken the laws of God's kingdom; if you were, that righteous anger would go in a very different direction. It would be the anger of grace, the anger of wisdom, the anger of instruction, and the anger of correction. No, you're angry because your children have broken the laws of your kingdom, and in your kingdom there shall be no parenting after 10:00. I am going to ask you to be honest about your anger and the ugly words that express it. How much of the anger that you have expressed in the situations and relationships of your daily life has had anything at all to do with the kingdom of God?

The Kingdom of Self and the Kingdom of God

Galatians 5 is very helpful here because it is a kingdom passage. The war between the two kingdoms—the kingdom of self and the kingdom of God—is being laid out in this little passage that applies the apostle Paul's discussion of the gospel to how we live:

> You, my brothers, were called to be free. But do not use your freedom to indulge the sinful nature; rather, serve one another in love. The entire law is summed up in a single command: "Love your neighbor as yourself." If you keep on biting and devouring each other, watch out or you will be destroyed by each other. (vv. 13–15 NIV)

The passage ends with a warning. We must never say that harsh, ugly, unloving, condemning, ungracious, selfish, prideful communication is okay. It's not okay. God has invested words with power. Nor must we say, "Yes, I was yelling at my husband, but he knows I love him," or, "I know I was ugly with my children this morning, but they know I care for them." Paul doesn't allow us to back away from the harvest of our words. Rather, Paul says, we must watch out or we will be consumed and destroyed by one another. Notice the words Paul uses: he doesn't say the relationship will be destroyed; he says *people* will be destroyed. You can crush the faith of people. You can destroy their hope. You can damage their identity. You can leave a legacy of darkness in the heart of others because of the evil of the communication that marked the relationship. What you say always produces some kind of harvest. What is the lasting legacy of your words?

But Paul does something helpful in this passage: he contrasts two overarching lifestyles, one of which is always ruling your heart and shaping your talk. The first lifestyle he characterizes with the phrase "indulge the sinful nature" (v. 13). It's a life driven by self-indulgent desire. It's a life that runs on the track of my wants, my needs, and my feelings; therefore, my words go wherever my desires take me. I may not know it, but I am living under the lordship of my desires. This, then, becomes the thing that structures my relationships with the people God has placed around me. What I really want from them is that they be the deliverers of my self-focused desires.

Reflect again on what 2 Corinthians 5:15 says about what sin does to us. If sin turns me in on myself so that all I live for is me, then sin in its essence is antisocial. Living for myself and the satisfaction of my selfish desires dehumanizes the people in my life. No longer are they people to me. No longer are they objects of my affection and service. No, my loved ones and friends are reduced either to vehicles to help me get what I want or to obstacles in the way of what I want. When they deliver what I want, I speak kindly to them, not actually because I love them but because I love myself and the fact that they have satisfied my desires. When they get in the way of what I want, I speak unkindly to them because I love myself, and they have made the mistake of getting in the way of what I crave.

Paul wants us to understand that God has bestowed us with his grace for something better. It is vital for each of us to understand that God didn't give us his grace to make our claustrophobic little kingdom function well. God gave us his grace to call us to the transforming glory of a better kingdom.

I would ask you again to be humbly honest with yourself. If I sat with you and listened to a recording of your words over the past month, whose kingdom, what kingdom, would I conclude those words were spoken to serve? Would it be the kingdom of self with its self-focused demands, expectancy, and entitlement? Would I hear someone quick to criticize, to judge, to slam, and to condemn because people are always violating the laws of your kingdom? Is the greatest moral offense in your life an offense that someone makes against the laws of your kingdom? When this happens, do you use words as a punishment or as a weapon? Do you use words to rein this person back into loyal service of the purposes of your kingdom of one?

Or would I hear you using words of love, honesty, encouragement, and service because your heart is taken up with the big-sky purposes of the kingdom of God? Paul writes, "The entire law is summed up in a single command" (v. 14a). If you had written that, what would you have written next? I probably would have written, "Love God above all else." But that is clearly not what Paul writes. He writes, "Love your neighbor as yourself" (v. 14b). That is an adequate summary of all that God calls us to.

It is important to get this truth, because it is only when I love God above all else that I will love my neighbor as myself. It's only when God is in the rightful place in my life that I will treat you with the love that I have received from him. Brothers and sisters, hear this: you don't first fix language problems, communication problems, and word problems horizontally; you first fix them vertically.

A Kingdom of Love

What kind of kingdom is the kingdom of God? It's a kingdom of boundless, glorious, powerful, and transforming love. What is the center event of the kingdom of God? It's a shocking sacrifice of redeeming love. You know nothing about the kingdom of God unless you understand that it is a kingdom of love. When you are filled with the glory of that love, when your heart is taken up by the mystery of that love, when what daily fills your heart is deep and worshipful gratitude for the miracle of divine love, then your words begin to be words of love, words of service, words of grace, words of encouragement, words of peace, and words that heal. When you wake up in the morning, no matter what's going on in your family, no matter what difficulty you are facing, and you can say, "How could it be that God would love me so much?" you will be free from the bondage to self-love.

This is going to bother some of you, but I think it's exactly what John says in 1 John. True love is not best propelled by duty. John says, "We love because he first loved us" (4:19 NIV). True love is propelled by gratitude. Think about me sliding next to my wife, Luella, on the couch, pulling her close and saying, "You know, Luella, I'm persuaded it is my responsibility to love you, and so I'm going to love you because I think it's what I'm supposed to do. I want you to know that I will do my duty." Luella probably wouldn't walk away saying, "I'm loved! I'm loved!" True biblical, big-kingdom love is motivated, initiated, and propelled by gratitude.

That leads us to a potentially uncomfortable question, but I am persuaded that it is a question that we need to ask: *What is this thing called love that is meant to drive my world of talk?* I am persuaded that much of what we call love just isn't love. Let me use marriage as an example. Maybe what a wife- and husband-to-be think is real love may not actually be love. It might be a woman who, not realizing the selfishness of her sinful nature, is actually shopping for a man whom she hopes will be the final piece of the puzzle of the dream that she has for her life. She shops through seemingly endless dating relationships until she finally finds him. She's amazed and excited that she has found the "perfect" man. She doesn't have to bend the tabs to make him fit into the puzzle of her life. He already fits right into the space. Could it be that she doesn't actually love this man? Could it be that she's attracted to him not because she loves him but because she loves herself? Could it be that she's excited that this man seems as if he will be the deliverer of all her claustrophobic, little kingdom-of-one dreams?

The problem, however, is that her future husband has been doing the same thing. Yes, they are powerfully attracted to each other, and that attraction is powerfully emotional, but it isn't true biblical love. That attraction is self-love masquerading as love for the other person. It doesn't take a PhD to predict what is going to happen in that marriage. Maybe it will take a day. Maybe it will take six months. Maybe it will take six years. But at some point there is going to be a horrible, discouraging, and disorienting collision of dreams because, contrary to what they thought, that man and woman didn't actually love one another; they loved themselves, and they were excited that the other was going to deliver their dream. When that didn't happen, the attraction gave way to irritation and to wondering why they ever wanted to marry each other in the first place.

Sometimes it doesn't take very long. I had a couple call me the day after I married them. The call actually came at 6:30 the next morning. Although they were very discouraged, I thought it was wonderful. I thought they were humble, perceptive, and intelligent. They had come to the end of their kingdom purposes quickly. They were ahead of the game. Their despair was a good thing. We were able that morning to begin to get their marriage running on the tracks of real God-centered, other-focused love.

What Is Love Anyway?

I want to turn your attention to 1 John 4:7–12, a biblical treatise on love. What is this love that is to propel our words?

> Beloved, let us love one another, for love is from God, and whoever loves has been born of God and knows God. Anyone who does not love does not know God, because God is love. In this the love of God was made manifest among us, that God sent his only Son into the world, so that we might live through him. In this is love, not that we have loved God but that he loved us and sent his Son to be the propitiation for our sins. Beloved, if God so loved us, we also ought to love one another. No one has ever seen God; if we love one another, God abides in us and his love is perfected in us.

You don't define love by a set of abstract concepts. Love is defined by an event, and that event is the cross of the Lord Jesus Christ. God calls us to cruciform love, that is, love that shapes itself to the cross of the Lord Jesus Christ. What is that love? I will give you a definition: *love is willing self-sacrifice for the redemptive good of another that doesn't demand reciprocation or that the person being loved is deserving.* That is the love that took Christ to the cross of his death for our redemption.

When I am filled with worshipful gratitude for the operation of the transforming love of the Lord Jesus Christ in my life—when this love becomes the glory of my life, when it becomes my deepest joy and my most powerful motivation, when it is the thing that gets me up in the morning and makes me rest at night, when it is my overarching paradigm—then I want to look for opportunities to somehow, someway be an agent of that transforming love. Oh, if just once in my life I could be a tool of that love, then every breath I take would be worth it.

In order to live this life of love, you and I need rescue. We don't need to be rescued from each other. We need to be rescued from ourselves, because as long as sin still lives inside of us, we sadly get re-attracted to our claustrophobic little kingdom of one. As long as sin still lives in us, we look at our wants, our needs, and our feelings as being more glorious than the expansive plans and purposes of the eternal kingdom of God. We still look to be satisfied with physical, created glories that do not have the capacity to fulfill us. They were created to be a finger pointing to the one glory that will only, ever satisfy: the glory of God. We still try to feed on glory that cannot fill the hunger of our hearts. So we need the moment-by-moment daily rescue of the grace of the Lord Jesus Christ. Without his rescuing grace, we would have no ability whatsoever to love another person in the way John describes.

What does all this have to do with your world of talk? Wholesome words of love and grace flow out of a heart that is ruled by this kind of love. Remember, you always speak out of the heart.

Does God's high calling of love and the purity of words that flow from it discourage you? Do you look at the people in your life in the situations and location in which you live and think there is no way you will be able to love people in that way or live up to God's standard and according to his design? Well, this final passage is for you. I want to encourage you with the words of 2 Peter 1. This passage is my friend. I don't know what I would do without these words:

> His divine power has granted to us all things that pertain to life and
> godliness, through the knowledge of him who called us [by] his own
> glory and excellence, by which he has granted to us his precious
> and very great promises [the Word of God], so that through them

you may become partakers of the divine nature, having escaped the corruption that is in the world because of sinful desire. (vv. 3–4)

"His divine power has granted . . ." If you're a grammarian, what's the tense of the verb? It's past perfect, a definitive action in the past with continuing results in the future. Therefore, if you are God's child, then what's promised is already in your storehouse. This is not a promise of what could be. This is a *redemptive is*; a statement of what is already yours. "His divine power has granted to us all things that pertain to life and godliness." Or as the NIV says, "everything we need for life and godliness."

Why does Peter use two words—life and godliness? I think Peter uses two words because he knows his audience. If he had said that God has given us everything that pertains solely to life, it would be very tempting to stick in the word *eternal*, so that we would say, "Isn't it wonderful that God is giving us everything we need so that some day we can live eternally with him?" That is a true and glorious fact, but it just doesn't happen to be Peter's topic here. So he uses a second word, *godliness*.

Godliness is a God-honoring life in thought, desire, word, and action. Between the time I come to Christ and the time I go home to be with him, God has already given me everything I need for that difficult conversation I'm having with my husband or my wife. He's given me everything I need to deal with that rebellious teenager in a way that reflects God's transforming grace. He's given me everything I need to talk to that irascible boss who never seems to respect me no matter how hard I work. He's given me everything I need to deal in graciousness and love with that neighbor who seems more concerned about boundaries than relationships. He's given me everything I need to have a difficult conversation with that person who has betrayed me. He's given me everything I need. Oh, that we would live out of this identity! Oh, that we would not be identity amnesiacs, living in the poverty of inability, when we have been made able by Christ.

What is the provision we have been given? First, it's the gift of God's *forgiveness*. Because of the substitutionary work of Christ, I can stand before my God one more time and say, "I'm such a mess. God, I get it wrong so often. I claim allegiance to your kingdom but

I slip back into that claustrophobic little kingdom of one. I again and again prize my agenda more than your glorious plan. Father, I cast myself before you once again. I say, 'Oh forgive me. Oh help me.'" Isn't it glorious that I can stand in all my weakness, in all my failure before a holy God, and be utterly unafraid because of what Jesus has done? I can run into his presence for his help one more time.

Second is the gift of *empowerment*. God knew that your need was so pervasive and expansive that he didn't just forgive you; he literally unzipped you and got inside you by his Spirit so that you have the power to do those things that he calls you to do. Consider this: Jesus is Immanuel not just because he came to earth; Jesus is Immanuel because he has made you the place where he dwells. God has dealt with your powerlessness, not just by giving you insightful commands and principles but by literally giving you himself. If you are God's child, he lives inside of you in power and glory, gracing you with what you need to obey his call.

But there is a third thing. God didn't just grant us forgiveness and enablement but ultimately *deliverance* as well. I don't know if you've thought about this, but you serve a dissatisfied Redeemer. He will not rest. He will not relent until every microbe of sin is eradicated from every cell of every heart of every one of his children. Some day we'll be invited to the one funeral that we all will want to attend: the funeral of sin. The promise of the gospel is that sin will die and we will be with Christ and will be like him in holiness forever and ever and ever.

By his grace, brothers and sisters, that glorious kingdom of transforming love is yours for the taking. Dear ones, the Father has chosen to grant you the kingdom. Why would you enter once again the claustrophobic confines of your little self-defined world?

Maybe you're thinking, "Paul, I get the principle, but how does it work?" Well, let me give you one final illustration. Imagine with me that you're a married man, and your wife is home with your three children. You head home, thinking that one of the things you love at the end of your day is that beautiful home-cooked meal. You can almost smell the smells as you're driving home. You recall that, as you left for work in the morning, you saw the beef roast shrink-wrapped in plastic on the counter, and you immediately had beefological visions. As you're driving home, you're thinking about that wonderful roast, but you arrive at home and come into the house, and the smells aren't so sweet. Your wife seems a little nervous and a little distant. As you sit down to eat, she puts a roast on the table in an act of embarrassment while mumbling an apology. The roast looks more like charcoal briquettes than beef. You look at her and say, "Do you know what I do for you? You know, I don't ask you for much. I'm a pretty tolerant guy. But the one thing that would be nice is if I could come home and have an edible meal." You point to the roast and say, "What do you expect me to do with that? You couldn't focus enough today to produce one decent meal for me? I don't get it. What did you do all day?"

That is the practical communication of the kingdom of self. What do you think is in the heart of that woman? Does she want to move toward you? Does she want to entrust herself to your care? Does she feel loved and encouraged? No, she doesn't. Remember Galatians 5:15: "If you bite and devour one another, watch out that you are not consumed by one another."

Let's wind the tape back to earlier in the day. You're smelling the beef in your mind as you drive home. But you come into the house, and the smells aren't very nice. Your wife, in an act of embarrassment, mumbles an apology as she puts the seared roast on the table. You grab her hand and say, "Dear, don't apologize. You have been such a sweet gift to me. You work so hard for this family. You love us dearly day after day. It is amazing to me that I live, with all my weakness and failure, with someone who faithfully loves me like you do. Hear me, dear: if all I have to deal with is a burnt roast, I'm an expansively blessed man. Don't apologize. I love you. It's okay." You have just read the loving words of a man whose heart is ruled by the kingdom of God.

What kingdom rules your words? Whose kingdom do you speak in service of—the claustrophobic kingdom of self or the big-sky country of the glorious, love-infused kingdom of God? The answer for most of us is probably both. Sometimes I get it right—sometimes I do find joy in the kingdom of God—and sometimes I get it very wrong. For the war between these two kingdoms that rages on the turf of my heart, I need the grace of the Lord Jesus Christ.

I have committed to pray three prayers each morning. The first one is a confession: "God, I'm a man in desperate need of help this morning." The second prayer is, "I pray in your grace that you would send your helpers my way." The third prayer is, "And I pray that you would give me the humility to receive the help that comes."

There is no escaping the message of Scripture: *word problems are heart problems*. There's an organic consistency between what is in my heart and what comes out of my mouth. The struggle of words is a struggle of kingdoms; a war between the kingdom of self and the kingdom of God. The kingdom that rules your heart will dictate your words. But there is grace—glorious, powerful, enabling, forgiving, and delivering grace—for this struggle. Remember, there is no more present or powerful argument for our daily moment-by-moment need of God's grace than the words that come out of our mouths. Each of us needs to be rescued by his grace. Each of us needs to be enflamed with love for his kingdom, with hearts filled with gratitude, so that we will speak as agents of his boundless transforming love. Pray for the rescue of his grace so that you may speak as he intended. That is a prayer you can be assured he will hear and answer.

CHAPTER TWO

The Bit, the Bridle, and the Blessing: An Exposition of James 3:1–12

Sinclair B. Ferguson

OUR FOCUS IN THIS STUDY is the teaching of James 3:1–12:

Not many of you should become teachers, my brothers, for you know that we who teach will be judged with greater strictness. For we all stumble in many ways, and if anyone does not stumble in what he says, he is a perfect man, able also to bridle his whole body. If we put bits into the mouths of horses so that they obey us, we guide their whole bodies as well. Look at the ships also: though they are so large and are driven by strong winds, they are guided by a very small rudder wherever the will of the pilot directs. So also the tongue is a small member, yet it boasts of great things.

How great a forest is set ablaze by such a small fire! And the tongue is a fire, a world of unrighteousness. The tongue is set among our members, staining the whole body, setting on fire the entire course of life, and set on fire by hell. For every kind of beast and bird, of reptile and sea creature, can be tamed and has been tamed by mankind, but no human being can tame the tongue. It is a restless evil, full of deadly poison. With it we bless our Lord and Father, and with it we curse people who are made in the likeness of God. From the same mouth come blessing and cursing. My brothers, these things ought not to be so. Does a spring pour forth from the same opening both fresh and salt water? Can a fig tree, my brothers, bear olives, or a grapevine produce figs? Neither can a salt pond yield fresh water.

James 3:1–12 contains the single most sustained discussion in the New Testament on the use of the tongue. I take the author of this little book to have been James, the half-brother of our Lord Jesus.[1] It is clear that he is steeped in the wisdom literature of the Old Testament Scriptures and also in the teaching of the Lord Jesus, to which his own teaching has many parallels. Both the book of Proverbs and our Lord Jesus spoke with searching clarity about the nature and use of the tongue. James walks in their footprints. Much of what he says is a powerful exposé of the sin and failure that mar our speech.

In this way James's words exemplify the central purposes of the teaching and preaching of God's Word. The resulting effect will be to "reprove, rebuke, and exhort" (2 Tim. 4:2). But James's message also exemplifies what Paul calls the profitability or usefulness of sacred Scripture: "teaching . . . correction . . . [child-]training."

In a word, the immediate focus of James's teaching—one might say the same of all apostolic teaching—is to bring Christian believers to maturity. Here, as well as in other places, he is completely in harmony with the way the apostle Paul employed all his God-given powers: "Him we proclaim, warning everyone and teaching everyone with all wisdom, that we may present everyone mature in Christ. For this I toil, struggling with all his energy that he powerfully works within me" (Col. 1:28–29).

In fact, this is one of James's burdens also. His five chapters constitute an extended piece of pastoral preaching, laced as it is with words of wisdom and warning. All along his goal is to lead his readers and hearers—men and women who were possibly once under his direct pastoral care but are now widely scattered—to full spiritual maturity, so that their whole being, without reservation, should be wholly Christ's.

We find that this motif runs through the entire book. As we come upon it in chapter 3, he has already shown (1) how spiritual maturity develops through response to suffering, and (2) how spiritual maturity is enhanced by response to the Word. Now he goes on to show that (3) spiritual maturity is evidenced by the use of the tongue. The mastery of it is one of the clearest marks of a whole person, a true Christian. Tongue-mastery is the fruit of self-mastery.

We will examine this teaching in order to accomplish three goals: (1) to "walk" through James 3:1–12 in order to feel the weight of its appeal; (2) to set this teaching in context of the whole book of James to discover that it is, in effect, only the tip of the iceberg of what he has to say about our speech; (3) to place these words in the broader gospel context that lies behind the book of James.

James 3:1–12 and Its Teaching on the Tongue

As we make our way into James 3:1–12, we notice it has a variety of basic driving principles.

The Difficulty of Taming the Tongue

James issues a special word of wise counsel to those who aspire to be teachers: "Not many of you should become teachers, my brothers, for you know that we who teach will be judged with greater strictness" (v. 1).

Why should this be? Teachers should be conscious of the weight and potential influence of what they say because words lie at the heart of the teaching ministry. To have an unreliable tongue is likely to provide a destructive model for those who are taught. The potential for multiplication of influence requires a canon of judgment that takes the measure of both responsibility and opportunity into account.

But James does not write as one who has "arrived." He is conscious of his own shortcomings: "for we all stumble in many ways" (v. 2). He has no false perfectionism. Perhaps he remembers how he misspoke about Jesus, demeaning him during the days of his ministry. Was James among those who said, "He is out of his mind" (Mark 3:21)? Was this one reason why our Lord visited him, in particular (as he did Simon Peter), after the resurrection (1 Cor. 15:7)?

But James's words are applicable far beyond those who are called to teach. We all use our tongues. If the mastery of the tongue is a sign of maturity, it is so for all Christians. So James 3:1–12 has general as well as specific application. How we use our tongues provides clear evidence of where we are spiritually.

When I was a child, our family physician used to ask us to stick out our tongues. (That was the only circumstance in which I was ever permitted to do that!) He seemed to be able to tell a great deal about our health by looking into our mouths. That is a parable of spiritual reality. What comes out of our mouths is usually an accurate index of the health of our hearts. Jesus said: "For out of the abundance of the heart the mouth speaks" (Matt. 12:34). So here, as a spiritual physician, James engages in a rigorous tongue analysis. James 3:1–12 is a veritable pathology laboratory in which analysis and diagnosis take place.

Notice James's axiom: the mature person is able to "bridle" his tongue. The person who can do this is master of the whole body.[2] The spiritual masters of the past understood this to have a double reference. The control of the tongue has both negative and positive aspects. It involves the ability to restrain the tongue in silence. But it also means being able to control it in gracious speech when that is required. Sanctification in any area of our lives always expresses this double dimension—a putting off and a putting on, as it were. Speech and silence, appropriately expressed, are together the mark of the mature.[3]

Nor is this James's first reference to speech. He had already noted that for a professing Christian to fail to bridle the tongue is to be guilty of self-deception (1:22–25) and the hallmark of a person whose religion is worthless (1:26). One might think here of the ease of speech but emptiness of weighty words in the life of John Bunyan's Mr. Talkative. He was all talk but no control, all words but without weight.

But with all of this said, James is forced into a confession. Nobody—Jesus excepted—has succeeded in mastering the tongue! Our only hope as we pursue the discipline of self that leads to mastery of the tongue is that we are Christ's and that we are being made increasingly like him. But this battle for vocal holiness is a long-running one, and it needs to be waged incessantly, daily, hourly.

Are we fighting it? We must seek to do so for a very important reason.

The Disproportionate Power of the Tongue

In James 3:3–5, James uses two commonplace but very vivid illustrations.

The tongue is like the bit in the mouth of a horse. This tiny appliance controls the enormous power and energy of the horse and is used to give it direction. James may well have been familiar with this picture from common experience in daily life. He had seen powerful Roman military horses and had probably heard stories of chariot races. The point, however, is the extraordinary power and influence concentrated in one small object. So it is with the tongue.

The tongue is also like the rudder in a boat. Large ships were not unknown in the ancient world. The ship that originally was to transport Paul across the Mediterranean en route to Rome held 276 people (Acts 27:37). We know that a large ship like the *Isis* could carry one thousand people. Yet such a capacious and heavy vessel was directed simply by a turn of the rudder! So it is with the tongue. The tongue is small. But its power, both for good and for ill, is out of all proportion to its size. "A fool's tongue," Bruce Waltke wryly notes, "is long enough to cut his own throat."[4]

Why does James speak this way? Presumably out of both biblical knowledge and personal experience. The tongue carries into the world the breath that issues from the heart.

Alas, we do not realize how powerful for evil the tongue is because we are so accustomed to its polluting influence. En route to give this address, I rode the hotel elevator with several others. On one floor the elevator stopped, the doors opened, and a woman entered the confined space. The doors closed, and I suspect everyone in the elevator almost instantaneously had the same thought: "She has been smoking!" In this confined "smoke-free" environment her breath could not be disguised.

So, says Jesus, the tongue projects the thoughts and intentions of the heart. It is from within, "out of the heart," that the mouth speaks (cf. Matt. 12:34; 15:18–19). But like the smoker, so accustomed to the odor, the atmosphere in which they live, the person with polluted speech has little or no sense of it—no sense that they exhale bad breath every time they speak.

Yet there is another side to this, a wonderfully encouraging side. Scripture teaches us that the breath by which we express our deepest desires, instincts, and opinions may produce helpful and pleasing fruit. Writes the wise man of Proverbs 15:4:

> A gentle tongue is a tree of life,
> but perverseness in it breaks the spirit.

So James sees that the tongue is an instrument of extraordinary power, out of all proportion to its size. Whatever its anatomical connections, its most significant connection is to the heart—whether hardened by sin or recreated by grace.

At this stage James is chiefly concerned that we should have a sense of the convicting power of his teaching. For this reason he began by addressing *the difficulty of taming the tongue*. It is a word spoken primarily to bring conviction of sin. For the tongue is difficult, indeed impossible, to tame naturally, because, as we have also seen, *it exercises power out of all proportion to its size*.

The Destruction Caused by the Tongue

Now, third, a series of vivid pictures flashes rapidly across James's mind as he thinks about the power of the tongue.

A Fire (v. 6). A small fire can destroy an entire forest; all it takes is an uncontrolled spark. So it is with the tongue. A sharp word, a loose sentence, a callous aside can cause a conflagration that cannot be extinguished. Words can consume and destroy a life.

James is very specific about the energy source for such destruction. The tongue that sets on fire is set on fire itself by hell. James uses the biblical term *Gehenna*—the background reference being to the Valley of Hinnom on the southern outskirts of Jerusalem. It served as the city dump—hence the reference to fire—which presumably constantly burned there to destroy garbage.[5] Was this the place to which our Lord's body would have been taken were it not for the thoughtfulness of Joseph of Arimathaea? If so, it is difficult not to share with James a sense of disgust. It is from such a hell that destructive words arise. Remember that imagery whenever similar words seek to force their way out of your mouth.

A World (v. 6). The tongue is "a world of unrighteousness." I remember reading a picture quiz in an in-flight magazine many years ago. Various things photographed from unusual angles were presented, and the challenge was to guess what the objects actually were. One seemed to be a striking photograph of the moon with all its craters—a dark world of death. Turning to check the answers I was astonished to find it was in fact a photograph of a human tongue! How appropriate that, when photographically magnified, it would appear like an entire world of death and darkness, full of dangerous craters.

A Stain (v. 6). The tongue is "set among our members, staining the whole body." How careful you are as you put on a dress for a wedding, especially if it is your own. How nervous about that new silk tie during dinner. The spot need only be a small one, but it ruins everything. So it is with the tongue and its words. No matter what graces you may have developed, if you have not gained tongue mastery, you can besmirch them all by an unguarded and ill-disciplined comment. Graces are fragile; therefore guard your tongue lest it destroy them.

A Restless Evil (v. 8). The unregenerate tongue roams the wilds, quick to defend itself, swift to attack others, anxious to subdue them, always marked by evil. It mimics Satan in this respect, who, having rebelled against the God of peace, can never settle. He goes to and fro throughout the earth (as in Job 1:7; 2:2), like a roaring lion seeking someone to devour (1 Pet. 5:8). The tongue that is under his lordship always shares that tendency. It has an inbuilt need to guard its own territory, to destroy rivals to itself, to be the king of the beasts.

A Deadly Poison (v. 8). James shares the perspective of Paul and, in turn, of the psalmist. The "venom of asps" is under the lips of sinners, "Their throat is an open grave; they use their tongues to deceive" (Rom. 3:13; Ps. 5:9). Whether suddenly or slowly, life is eaten away and destroyed. Perhaps here there is an echo of Genesis 3 and the deadly deceit of Eve by the serpent—with all its deadly and hellish consequences.

James, however unbelieving he might have been during Jesus' early ministry, has clearly absorbed his half brother's teaching and has been led by it to the multitude of Old Testament word pictures about the power and destructive ability of the tongue. If the pen is mightier than the sword, it is equally true that we can kill a man as easily with the words we use as with a physical weapon (Matt. 5:21–22).

Of course, all this is naturally true of the unregenerate man. The tragedy is—and it is this tragedy that surely concerns James here—that the same destructive powers may be released within the believing community.

I sometimes wonder if this is a distinctively evangelical sin. Of

course it is by no means exclusively so. But how commonplace it
seems to be to hear a fellow Christian's name mentioned in some context or other, and the first words of response demean his reputation,
belittle him, and distance him from acceptance into the fellowship,
although this is a brother for whom Christ died!

The saintly Robert Murray M'Cheyne was surely nearer the mark
when he resolved that when a fellow Christian's name was mentioned
in company, if he could not say anything good about him, he would
refrain from all speech about him. Better that, surely, than to be careless with fire and "destroy a brother for whom Christ died" (Rom.
14:15; 1 Cor. 8:11).

The young Jonathan Edwards penned a number of his *Resolutions*
around this theme. They are worth noting:

> 31. *Resolved*, Never to say anything at all against any body, but
> when it is perfectly agreeable to the highest degree of Christian
> honor, and of love to mankind, agreeable to the lowest humility,
> and sense of my own faults and failings, and agreeable to the golden
> rule; often, when I have said anything against any one, to bring it
> to, and try it strictly by, the test of this Resolution.
>
> 34. *Resolved*, In narrations never to speak anything but the pure
> and simple verity.
>
> 36. *Resolved*, Never to speak evil of any, except I have some
> particular good call to it.
>
> 70. Let there be something of benevolence in all that I speak.[6]

How easily the failure to master the tongue can destroy the effect of
every grace that had taken years to build into our lives! Introduce
poison here and we endanger everything.

A seminary colleague once told me how, because of flight delays,
he arrived late and very weary at a hotel where he had booked a room.
The young desk clerk could find no reservation under his name. My
weary friend, who had had a miserable day, lost some self-control and
started a small verbal blaze around the unfortunate employee, as if the
problem were of the young man's making. Having found him a room
the clerk invited him to fill in the guest form. My colleague included
the name of the theological seminary at which we both taught. As the
clerk looked at the form he gasped: "Are you from *the* Westminster

Seminary?" he asked, and then said excitedly, "This is amazing. I have just recently become a Christian. I have heard about your seminary! How amazing, and marvelous to meet you! Wow, are you really from Westminster Seminary?"

The story could so easily have ended on a different note: a stain inflicted on a young man by a mature believer—a stain that might have proved impossible to wash out. We have all seen or caused moments like this. The tongue can be the most powerful, destructive member in the entire body.

In this connection it is salutary to remember the thrust of Paul's most basic and powerful presentation of our need for the gospel. "Whatever the law says it speaks to those who are under the law, *so that every mouth may be stopped*" (Rom. 3:19).

I still recall the shivers that went down my spine on first reading, in 1970, D. Martyn Lloyd-Jones's exposition of these words:

> Paul now points out . . . that when you realize what the Law is truly saying to you the result is that "every mouth shall be stopped." You are rendered speechless. You are not a Christian unless you have been made speechless! How do you know whether you are a Christian or not? It is that you "stop talking." The trouble with the non-Christian is that he goes on talking. . . .
>
> How do you know whether a man is a Christian? The answer is that his mouth is "shut." I like this forthrightness of the Gospel. People need to have their mouths shut, "stopped." . . . You do not begin to be a Christian until your mouth is shut, is stopped, and you are speechless and have nothing to say.[7]

There is a "something"—almost indefinable—about the person who has clearly been converted to Christ. Dr. Lloyd-Jones surely put his finger on the essence of it—the humbling of the proud, self-sufficient heart, the breaking of our native arrogance. Our tongues are so often the most obvious index of that ungodly drive at the center of our being. But the slaying of inner pride and the illumination of our minds in regeneration create a new disposition and affection. The true convert will have a Jacob-like limp in his speech as well as in his walk—because in spiritual anatomy (as distinct from physical anatomy), the heart and the tongue are directly connected to each other. The subduing of the heart leads to the silencing of the tongue; humility within leads to humility expressed. Only when we have been thus silenced are we in any position to begin to speak. And when we do, by God's grace, we speak as those who have first been silenced.

The Deadly Inconsistency That Plagues the Tongue

James is not yet finished with his devastating analysis of the tongue. He draws attention to a fourth characteristic as the analysis now rises to a crescendo of exposure:

> No human being can tame the tongue. . . . With it we bless our Lord and Father, and with it we curse people who are made in the likeness of God. From the same mouth come blessing and cursing. My brothers, these things ought not to be so. Does a spring pour forth from the same opening both fresh and salt water? Can a fig tree, my brothers, bear olives, or a grapevine produce figs? Neither can a salt pond yield fresh water. (James 3:8–12)

I am reminded of the old cowboy-and-Indian movies my parents used to take me to when I was a child. There is only one line I recall an Indian ever speaking, but it was so frequently repeated it became engraved as one of my earliest memories of childhood: "White man speak with forked tongue." It was meant as, and really was, a damning indictment.

James shared that perspective but brought to it a more profound analysis: "Forked tongue connected to forked heart." Such speech is a mark of the "double-minded man" who is "unstable in all his ways" (James 1:8). It is not an amiable weakness. It expresses a damnable contradiction in our very being. It is an "ought not to be," like a spring that spouts forth both fresh and salt water. It is more contradictory than anything we find in nature, like a fig tree bearing olives, a grapevine producing figs, a salt pond yielding fresh water.

Notice the power of James's own words. Do not try to parry the blow. His words are intended to be a sharp two-edged sword "piercing to the division of soul and of spirit, of joints and marrow, and discerning the thoughts and intentions of the heart" (Heb. 4:12).

We were created as the image of God to bless God. It is blatant hypocrisy, double-mindedness, and sin to bless God and then casually curse those who have been made as his very likeness. But the forked tongue of the double-minded person enslaves him or her. He or she thinks the unthinkable and speaks unspeakable contradictions. James is blood earnest as he rips up the consciences of his contemporary readers, many of whom were, perhaps, once members of his dear flock in Jerusalem before being scattered abroad.

If such words could be spoken to professing Christians serious enough in their faith to experience persecution and suffer privation in a world that was becoming increasingly inhospitable to the followers of the Way—how much more devastating are they when addressed to pampered, often self-indulgent professors of Christianity in the early twenty-first century?

But now that our consciences have been, to use Puritan language, "ripped up," a question arises. Why does James apparently give no practical counsel about *how* we are to deal with the tongue? Are we left to go to the local Christian bookstore, or attend a seminar or conference, in order to know how to sanctify the use of the tongue? Why is there no practical counsel?

But in fact there is—if we will only stay with James long enough to hear it. Indeed, whenever there is such analysis in the New Testament letters there is ordinarily practical counsel written into the teaching itself. True, it may not be immediately evident, but if we keep our minds and spirits in the passage long enough and learn to wait patiently on the Lord in his Word, it will become clear. Even where there are no obvious imperatives to tell us what to do next, they are almost invariably implied in the text, woven as it were into its very warp and woof, underlining for us that it is by *the Word itself* and not by ourselves that we are sanctified. Did not James's brother pray "sanctify them in [or by] the truth; your word is truth" (John 17:17)?

In order to help us to grasp how James does this, it will be helpful, further, to consider how this teaching fits in with the rest of the book.

James 3:1–12 in the Context of the Entire Book

We are told in the sacred record that when Job felt himself to be under special pressure in his sufferings (and, unknown to him, under the specific assault of the Devil to destroy his enjoyment of God) he made "a covenant with [his] eyes" in order thus to bind on his heart the pattern of holiness he needed to develop (see Job 31:1ff.). Guarding the eyes implied guarding eyes in the heart as well as in the head.

Temptation, and therefore spiritual compromise, often find their easiest access route to the heart via the eyes. By the same token, sin may find its easiest exit route from our hearts via the mouth. The exhortation of Proverbs to "keep your heart with all vigilance" is immediately followed by an exhortation to "put away from you crooked speech, and put devious talk far from you" (Prov. 4:23–24). Guarding the heart involves guarding the tongue. To apply Job's principle to our present subject, we need to learn to say, "I will make a covenant with my tongue."

Rather wonderfully, this is what James helps us to do throughout his letter. Perhaps, in the context of a book coming from a Desiring God conference, we may be permitted to take a leaf out of Jonathan Edwards's *Resolutions* and express the burden of the practical exhortations implicit in James in a similar fashion.

Here, then, are twenty resolutions on the use of the tongue to which the letter's teaching gives rise:

1) *Resolved: To ask God for wisdom to speak and to do so with a single mind.*

"If any of you lacks wisdom, let him ask God, who gives generously to all without reproach, and it will be given him. . . . in faith with no doubting. . . . For that person must not suppose that he will receive anything . . . he is a double-minded man, unstable in all his ways" (James 1:5–8).

2) *Resolved: To boast only in my exaltation in Christ or my humiliation in the world.*

"Let the lowly brother boast in his exaltation, and the rich in his humiliation, because like a flower of the grass he will pass away" (James 1:9–10).

3) *Resolved: To set a watch over my mouth.*

"Let no one say when he is tempted, 'I am being tempted by God,' for God cannot be tempted with evil, and he himself tempts no one" (James 1:13).

4) *Resolved: To be constantly quick to hear, slow to speak.*

"Know this, my beloved brothers: let every person be quick to hear, slow to speak, slow to anger" (James 1:19).

5) *Resolved: To learn the gospel way of speaking to the poor and the rich.*

"My brothers, show no partiality as you hold the faith in our Lord Jesus Christ, the Lord of glory. For if a man wearing a gold ring and fine clothing comes into your assembly, and a poor man in shabby clothing also comes in, and if you pay attention to the one who wears the fine clothing and say, 'You sit here in a good place,' while you say to the poor man, 'You stand over there,' or, 'Sit down at my feet,' have you not then made distinctions among yourselves and become judges with evil thoughts?" (James 2:1–4).

6) *Resolved: To speak in the consciousness of the final judgment.*

"So speak and so act as those who are to be judged under the law of liberty" (James 2:12).

7) *Resolved: To never stand on anyone's face with words that demean, despise, or cause despair.*

"If a brother or sister is poorly clothed and lacking in daily food, and one of you says to them, 'Go in peace, be warmed and filled' without giving them the things needed for the body, what good is that?" (James 2:15–16).

8) *Resolved: To never claim a reality I do not experience.*

"If you have bitter jealousy and selfish ambition in your hearts, do not boast and be false to the truth" (James 3:14).

9) *Resolved: To resist quarrelsome words as marks of a bad heart.*

"What causes quarrels and what causes fights among you? Is it not this, that your passions are at war within you?" (James 4:1).

10) *Resolved: To never speak evil of another.*

"Do not speak evil against one another, brothers. The one who speaks against a brother or judges his brother, speaks evil against the law and judges the law. But if you judge the law, you are not a doer of the law but a judge" (James 4:11).

11) *Resolved: To never boast in what I will accomplish.*

"Come now, you who say, 'Today or tomorrow we will go into such and such a town and spend a year there and trade and make a profit'—yet you do not know what tomorrow will bring. What is your life? For you are a mist that appears for a little time and then vanishes" (James 4:13).

12) *Resolved: To always speak as one who is subject to the providences of God.*

"Instead you ought to say, 'If the Lord wills, we will live and do this or that'" (James 4:15).

13) *Resolved: To never grumble, knowing that the Judge is at the door.*

"Do not grumble against one another, brothers, so that you may not be judged; behold, the Judge is standing at the door" (James 5:9).

14) *Resolved: To never allow anything but total integrity in my speech.*

"But above all, my brothers, do not swear, either by heaven or by earth or by any other oath, but let your 'yes' be yes and your 'no' be no, so that you may not fall under condemnation" (James 5:12).

15) *Resolved: To speak to God in prayer whenever I suffer.*

"Is anyone among you suffering? Let him pray" (James 5:13).

16) *Resolved: To sing praises to God whenever I am cheerful.*

"Is anyone cheerful? Let him sing praise" (James 5:13).

17) *Resolved: To ask for the prayers of others when I am sick.*

"Is anyone among you sick? Let him call for the elders of the church, and let them pray over him, anointing him with oil in the name of the Lord" (James 5:14).

18) *Resolved: To confess it whenever I have failed.*

"Therefore, confess your sins to one another" (James 5:16).

19) *Resolved: To pray for one another when I am together with others in need.*

"Pray for one another, that you may be healed" (James 5:16).

20) *Resolved: To speak words of restoration when I see another wander.*

"My brothers, if anyone among you wanders from the truth and someone brings him back, let him know that whoever brings back a sinner from his wandering will save his soul from death and will cover a multitude of sins" (James 5:19–20).

Will we so resolve?

Finally, we turn to consider this passage in the context of the gospel.

James 3:1–12 in the Context of the Whole Gospel

When we take one step back from James 3:1–12 and read it in the context of the entire letter, we discover that James's searing analysis is surrounded by the most practical counsel to enable us to master the tongue and to speak well for God.

When we take another step back and view his words through the wide-angle lens of the biblical gospel, we are able all the more clearly to understand and appreciate what James is "doing" when he speaks as he does.

As is well known, in his early days as a reformer, Martin Luther thought that James was "an epistle full of straw":

> In sum the gospel and the first epistle of St. John, St. Paul's epistles, especially those to the Romans, Galatians, and Ephesians; and St. Peter's first epistle, are the books that show Christ to you. They teach everything you need to know for your salvation, even if you were never to see or hear any other book or hear any other teaching. In comparison with these, the epistle of St. James is an epistle full of straw, because it contains nothing evangelical.[8]

He would later think better of it. For the truth is that James's teaching cannot be rightly interpreted without realizing that it is rooted in the teaching of and energized by the grace of "faith in our Lord Jesus Christ, the Lord of glory" (James 2:1).

In that light we can discern a profoundly gospel-centered pattern in what James is seeking to accomplish as a pastor of the souls of his readers. His gospel method is in three steps.

1) Realize That the Depth of Your Sin, the Pollution of Your Heart, and Your Need of Saving Grace Are All Evidenced in Your Use of the Tongue

This is the method of grace from beginning to end. It is nowhere more starkly illustrated than in the experience of Isaiah. There is no more powerful passage in the Old Testament than Isaiah 6; but it is often read as if it were detached from Isaiah 1–5. By reading it in isolation we inevitably miss a very clear pattern into which it fits.

Isaiah has been ripping up the consciences of his sinful contemporaries. He does so in a series of six woe pronouncements (Isa. 5:8, 11, 18, 20, 21, 22). God's holy anger burns against them (5:25). Like a shepherd whistling for his dogs to come to tend the sheep, Yahweh will call on the nations to come as his servants, with arrows sharp as flint, with horses' hoofs like flint, with roaring like a lion. Darkness and distress will ensue—the terrible judgment of the Holy One of Israel (Isa. 5:26–30). But for the sensitive Bible reader the appearance of *six* woes creates an expectation that a climactic *seventh* woe is about to be pronounced. Against whom will Isaiah pronounce the ultimate woe?

The answer follows in chapter six. The prophet meets with the exalted God whose majestic presence seems to flood the temple. Isaiah sees creatures who are perfectly and perpetually holy cover their faces before the glory of the One who is eternally, infinitely, inherently, uncreatedly holy. Everything around Isaiah seems to be disintegrating. Everything within him seems to come apart. He is "lost," or "ruined" (Isa. 6:5). The language expresses the stunned silence felt in the presence of major disaster or death.[9] This is Isaiah's "twin towers" day, the 9/11 moment in his spiritual experience. From his assumed security he had pronounced six devastating maledictions. Now he realizes that the last and climactic woe must be pronounced against—himself! And why? "Woe is me! For I am lost; for *I am a man of unclean lips*, and I dwell in the midst of a people of unclean lips; for my eyes have seen the King, the LORD of hosts!" (Isa. 6:5).

In whimsical moments I think I can see Isaiah as he staggers into the house of his friend Benjamin later that day, ashen faced, shaken to the roots by his experience. He blurts out fragmentary details of his vision of the Holy One of Israel (the title that hereafter will be his preferred way of describing the Lord). He has discovered he is a "man of unclean lips."

I think I can hear dear Benjamin reply sympathetically—worried that his friend of many years is becoming unstable: "Not you, Isaiah; you are the last person of whom that is true. You are our most prominent and most eloquent preacher."

I think I hear Isaiah say in response, "You do not understand. I have seen the King. I have felt the pollution on my tongue. The light has exposed the darkness in its every crevice. Alas for me, it is in the very instrument God has called me to use, in the very area of my life in which others call me 'gifted,' that sin has most deeply entangled itself. I am a wretched man! Woe, woe, woe is me!"

We foolishly assume that our real struggles with sin are in the areas where we are "weak." We do not well understand the depth of sin until we realize that it has made its home far more subtly where we are "strong," and in our gifts rather than in our weaknesses and inadequacies. It is in the very giftedness God has given that sin has been at its most perverse and subtle!

But when we are brought to see this, stripped bare of our layers of self-deceit, and led to repentance, then God may make something of us.

Many—although I do not number myself among them—seem to find speech easy. Recent generations have, after all, been educated to be able to speak, to contribute to discussion and debate, to express themselves by the spoken word rather than by writing (as was true of my generation—at least in my native land of Scotland).

It rarely seems to strike us that it is precisely here, therefore, in our speech, that sin is most likely to abound.

Only when we have been brought to such a recognition do we realize how dangerous and destructive our tongues have been. Only then do we cry out to God in repentance and run to him with tears to seek forgiveness in the gospel.

Then we need to grasp a second principle.

2) Recognize That You Are a New Creation in Christ

At the beginning of his argument, James had urged his hearers, "You need to recognize that you have become a new creation in Christ Jesus, indeed a kind of firstfruits of his creation" (cf. 1:18). I may not yet be that mature man I want to be. But thank God that I am not the old man that I once was!

What a great way to think about an ordinary Christian life! We live in a created order marred by sin. That sin has twisted and polluted our speech. But God has begun his work of new creation and has inaugurated aspects of it that will be consummated when Jesus Christ returns. Then in the "regeneration" of all things (Matt. 19:28, NASB),[10] every tongue will confess that Jesus Christ is Lord.

But notice carefully how God regenerates us: "Of his own will he brought us forth by the word of truth, that we should be a kind of firstfruits of his creation." Regeneration is a sovereign work of God, yes; but it does not ordinarily take place in a vacuum. Since it involves having our eyes opened to see the kingdom of God (John 3:3), God ordinarily regenerates us in the context of the truth of the gospel illuminating our minds. Truth in the mind forms truth in the heart, the very thing for which David prayed (Ps. 51:10), and which he realized would lead in turn to transformed speech:

> Then I will teach transgressors your ways,
>   and sinners will return to you.
> Deliver me from bloodguiltiness, O God,
>   O God of my salvation,
>   and my tongue will sing aloud of your righteousness.
> O Lord, open my lips,
>   and my mouth will declare your praise. (Ps. 51:13–15)

How important for us to recognize the power of new birth to create new affections, which in turn come to expression in the new speech patterns of the gospel!

3) Continue in the Word

The work of the Word inaugurates the Christian life, but it also sustains its progress. My tongue is ongoingly cleansed and transformed by (if I may so express it) what comes from God's tongue. As the heart hears with open ears the Word of God again and again, it is renewed and begins to produce a transformed tongue. The principle is this: what comes out of our mouths is more and more determined by what has come out of "the mouth of God." The sanctification of the tongue is a work in us that is driven by the Word of God coming to us as we hear it and indwelling us as we receive it.

This was the "secret" of the Lord Jesus' own use of his tongue. Matthew sees our Lord Jesus as fulfilling the prophecy of the first of the Servant Songs in the second half of the prophecy of Isaiah:

> He will not quarrel or cry aloud,
>   nor will anyone hear his voice in the streets;
> a bruised reed he will not break,
>   and a smoldering wick he will not quench. (Matt. 12:19–20, quoting Isa. 42:2–3)

If we ask how this was true in his life, the answer is found in the third Servant Song:

The Lord GOD has given me
    the tongue of those who are taught,
that I may know how to sustain with a word
    him who is weary.
Morning by morning he awakens;
    he awakens my ear
    to hear as those who are taught.
The Lord GOD has opened my ear,
    and I was not rebellious;
    I turned not backward.
I gave my back to those who strike,
    and my cheeks to those who pull out the beard;
I hid not my face
    from disgrace and spitting. (Isa. 50:4–6)

The most important single aid to my ability to use my tongue for the glory of Jesus is allowing the Word of God to dwell in me so richly that I cannot speak with any other accent. When I do, the result is "teaching and admonishing one another in all wisdom, singing. . . . And . . . in word or deed, do[ing] everything in the name of the Lord Jesus, giving thanks to God the Father" (Col. 3:16–17).

That, incidentally (although it is *not* an incidental matter) is why it is so important to be under a ministry of the Word where the Scriptures are expounded with the grace and power of the Holy Spirit. It is by this means—yes, with private study—that the Word of God begins to do its own spiritual work in us. As words that have been formed in God's mouth are digested as the bread of life by us, they begin to form our thinking, affections, and volitions in a wonderful way.

Too many Christians fall into the trap of believing that God gives regeneration and justification, but then we are essentially left to our own efforts to do the rest. We need to see that we live by every word that comes out of God's mouth. God's Word sanctifies us. The more I awake in the morning and feed myself with the Scriptures and the more I am saturated with the Word under a biblical ministry, the more the word of Christ will do the sanctifying work in me and on me, and consequently the more Christ will train my tongue as his Word molds and shapes me. Yes, there needs to be rigorous activity—but it is in order to "let the word of Christ dwell in you richly." It is a receptive activity!

In this, as Isaiah's song teaches us, our Savior is our Exemplar. But he is not only, nor is he first of all, an exemplar. To be that, he needed first to become our Savior. All this is part of the grand vision of Isaiah's Servant Songs (so influential in Jesus' own reception of God's Word). The Father opened the ear of his Son; the Son was not rebellious. He was willing to be "oppressed and afflicted." As he experienced this in his trial and condemnation, "he opened not his mouth" (Isa. 53:7).

Why was Jesus silent? Is there more to this than meets the eyes? Indeed there is! He was silent because of every word that has proceeded from your lips; because of every word that provides adequate reason for God to damn you for all eternity, because you have cursed him or his image.

The Lord Jesus came into the world to bear the judgment of God against the sin of our tongues. When he stood before the high priest and the judgment seat of Pontius Pilate, he accepted a sentence of guilt. But that was my guilt. He bore in his body on the tree the sins of my lips and my tongue.

Do you wish you could control your tongue better? Do you want to follow the example of Jesus? Then you need to understand that he is Savior first, and then he is Example. You need to come, conscious of the sin of your lips, and say:

> God, be merciful to me, a sinner.
> I thank you that Jesus came and was silent
> in order that he might bear the penalty of all my misuse of
> my tongue.

And when you know that he has taken God's judgment and wrath against your every sinful word, you cannot but come to him and say:

> "O, for a thousand tongues to sing my great Redeemer's praise."

He is able to answer that prayer, and its companion petition:

> "Be of sin the double cure, cleanse me from its guilt and power."

All the guilt can be cleansed away! Christ can deliver you from the misuse of the tongue. And when you come to him conscious of that sin, you discover what a glorious Savior he is. Delivered, albeit not yet perfected and glorified, your tongue now shows forth his praises. Taken out of the pit and from the miry clay, on your lips is now a new song of praise to your God. Then people not only hear a different vocabulary, but they hear you speak with a different accent. That is what leaves the lasting impression of the power of Christ and the transformation of grace in your life.

My native land is Scotland. I have the privileged status of being a resident alien in the United States. I carry a green card. But people often remind me, "You have an accent." (That said, it is one of the wonderful things about the presence and work of Christ's Spirit in preaching that, fifteen minutes into the exposition, it is possible that others cease to notice the accent and hear only *his* accent.)

Being "afflicted," therefore, with an "accent," brief elevator rides—and the usual brief conversations that ensue there—often give me a certain mischievous pleasure. As the doors open at my floor and I step out, someone will occasionally call, "You have an accent. Where do you come from?" As I watch the doors begin to close, I say with a smile, "Columbia, South Carolina," and watch the puzzled faces whose expression says, "Come on! You're not from around here . . . are you?"

That is surely a parable of what it is possible for the people of God to become in the way we use our tongues, as by God's grace we learn to speak with a Jesus-like accent.

At the end of the day, it may not be so much what people say to you when you are in a room that is the really telling thing about your speech as a Christian. Rather it may be the questions people ask when you leave the room. "Where does he come from?" "Do you know where she belongs?"

Do you speak like someone who "sounds" a little like Jesus because, born broken in your consciousness of your sinful tongue, you have found pardon and renewal in Christ, and now his Word dwells richly in you?

At the end of the day, that is what spiritual maturity looks like— or better, sounds like—because of the transformation of our use of the tongue.

May that be true of us more and more!

CHAPTER THREE

Is There Christian Eloquence? Clear Words and the Wonder of the Cross

John Piper

IS THERE CHRISTIAN ELOQUENCE? I begin by showing why this question is urgent for me, and in the process I hope to clarify what the question means and what eloquence means. The question is urgent first and foremost because the apostle Paul, writing under the inspiration of the Holy Spirit, says in 1 Corinthians 1:17, "Christ did not send me to baptize but to preach the gospel, and *not with words of eloquent wisdom,* lest the cross of Christ be emptied of its power." Christ sent Paul to preach, *not with eloquence,* lest the cross be gutted. That's why I am asking the question, *Is there Christian eloquence?*

Even if you use the NIV ("not with words of human wisdom") or the NASB ("not in cleverness of speech") or the KJV ("not with wisdom of words"), the point remains the same. There is a way to speak the gospel—a way of eloquence or cleverness or human wisdom—that nullifies the cross. I dread nullifying the cross, and therefore it is urgent that I know what this eloquence-cleverness-wisdom of words is—so I can avoid it.

Or consider 1 Corinthians 2:1, where Paul says, "And I, when I came to you, brothers, did not come proclaiming to you the testimony of God *with lofty speech or wisdom.*" Or the NIV: "I did not come with *eloquence or superior wisdom.*" Or the NASB: "I did not come with *superiority of speech or of wisdom.*" Or the KJV: "[I] came not with *excellency of speech* or of wisdom.*"

For a pastor, or anyone who wants to speak the gospel to others without emptying the cross of its power, this is an urgent issue. If I choose words, or ways of putting words together, or ways of delivering them, with a view to increasing their life-giving, pride-humbling, God-exalting, Christ-magnifying, joy-intensifying, love-awakening, missions-mobilizing, justice-advancing impact, am I doing with my word selection and word arrangement and word delivery what is only supposed to be done by the cross of Christ, and so emptying it of its power?

In other words, is Paul saying that the pursuit of impact on others through word selection, word arrangement, and word delivery pre-empts Christ's power and belittles the glory of the cross? Answering this is urgent for any of us who would speak or write about the truths of the gospel.

Is the Bible Eloquent?

Complicating the question is this: most Bible scholars throughout history have drawn attention to the fact that the Bible itself has many eloquent parts. For example, John Calvin said, "Let us pay attention to the style of Isaiah, which is not only pure and elegant, but also is ornamented with high art—from which we may learn that eloquence may be of great service to faith."[1]

Or similarly consider what the poet John Donne said: "The Holy Ghost in penning the Scriptures delights himself, not only with a propriety, but with a delicacy, and harmony, and melody of language; with height of Metaphors, and other figures, which may work greater impressions upon the Readers."[2] In other words, Donne is saying that there is eloquence of language in the Bible, and some of the impact of the text on readers is owing in some way to that eloquence.

Is There Spirit-led Eloquence? → "Abba, Father"

Consider what Martin Luther says on Galatians 4:6: "The Spirit makes intercession for us not with many words or long prayer, but only with a groaning . . . a little sound and a feeble groaning, as 'Ah,

Father!' . . . Wherefore, this little word 'Father' . . . passes all the eloquence of Demosthenes, Cicero, and of the most eloquent rhetoricians that ever were in the world."[3] So Luther says the Holy Spirit himself leads us at times to a kind of eloquence—even in prayer.

So if these observations of Calvin, Luther, and Donne are right, what did Paul mean when he said he renounced eloquence for the sake of the cross? Or are Calvin and Luther and Donne missing something?

The Eloquence of George Whitefield

Another way to feel the urgency of the question, *Is there Christian eloquence?* is to compare what was said about two giants of the first Great Awakening, George Whitefield and Jonathan Edwards. These two men were deeply unified theologically yet significantly different in the way they preached.

In the spring of 1740, George Whitefield was in Philadelphia preaching outdoors to thousands of people. Benjamin Franklin attended most of these messages. Franklin, who did not believe what Whitefield was preaching, commented on these perfected sermons:

> His delivery . . . was so improved by frequent repetition, that every accent, every emphasis, every modulation of voice, was so perfectly well turned, and well placed, that *without being interested in the subject, one could not help being pleased with the discourse*: a pleasure of much the same kind with that received from an excellent piece of music.[4]

Here is preaching that is so eloquent you can like it without believing anything in it. In other words, the language itself—the word selection, word arrangement, and word delivery—was such that it was pleasurable to Franklin, who cared nothing for what the language meant. Franklin loved his eloquence and rejected the cross. Was Whitefield emptying the cross of its power?

Eloquence in Our Day

And just in case you're among the generation of younger preachers who don't give a fig about this so-called eloquence and think you have this one solved because you don't care about that kind of eloquence—beware. There is an "eloquence" of "hip" and "dress"

and "slang" and "savvy" and "casual" and the "appearance of art-
lessness" that can have the exact same mesmerizing effect in our day
that Whitefield's eloquence had in his: people like it without sharing
any of the convictions. In other words, none of us escapes the urgency
of this question. We all need an answer.

The Eloquence of Jonathan Edwards

But now consider Jonathan Edwards, Whitefield's contemporary
and friend. Edwards did not receive such accolades for dramatic eloquence as Whitefield. But he did have another kind of eloquence. One
eyewitness answered the question whether Edwards was an eloquent
preacher like this:

> If you mean, by eloquence, what is usually intended by it in our cit-
> ies; he had no pretensions to it. He had no studied varieties of the
> voice, and no strong emphasis. He scarcely gestured, or even moved;
> and he made no attempt, by the elegance of his style, or the beauty of
> his pictures, to gratify the taste, and fascinate the imagination. But, if
> you mean by eloquence, the power of presenting an important truth
> before an audience, with overwhelming weight of argument, and
> with such intenseness of feeling, that the whole soul of the speaker
> is thrown into every part of the conception and delivery; so that the
> solemn attention of the whole audience is riveted, from the begin-
> ning to the close, and impressions are left that cannot be effaced; Mr.
> Edwards was the most eloquent man I ever heard speak.[5]

In either case—Whitefield the dramatic orator or Edwards the
motionless, intense logician—the question remains: were these forms
of eloquence an emptying of the cross of Christ? Were they following
Paul's example when he said that he preached the gospel "not with
words of eloquent wisdom, lest the cross of Christ be emptied of its
power"?

James Denney's Haunting Statement

There is a statement that James Denney made over a hundred years
ago that haunts me. Whether we are talking about the more high-
brow eloquence of oratory or the more low-brow, laid-back, cool
eloquence of anti-oratory, Denney's statement cuts through to the

ultimate issue. He said, "No man can give the impression that he himself is clever and that Christ is mighty to save."[6] This has been one of the most influential sentences I have ever read regarding how we talk about Christ. Does this mean that any conscious craft or art in writing or speaking elevates self and obscures the truth that Christ is mighty to save?

Is Eloquence an End in Itself?

There is one last angle that shows the urgency of this question: *Is there Christian eloquence?* The journal *Books and Culture* published a review of a book by Denis Donoghue, professor of English and American Letters at New York University. The title of his book is *On Eloquence.* I was so aggravated by the review that I got the book and read it over the summer.

Donoghue's contention is that eloquence is a surprising, impacting style that is an end in itself. He says, for example,

> A speech or an essay may be eloquent, but if it is, the eloquence is incidental to its aim. Eloquence, as distinct from rhetoric, has no aim: it is a play of words or other expressive means. . . . The main attribute of eloquence is gratuitousness.[7]
> . . . Eloquence does not serve a purpose or an end in action. . . . In rhetoric, one is trying to persuade someone to do something: in eloquence, one is discovering with delight the expressive resources of the means at hand.[8]

He agrees with (and quotes) E. M. Cioran that this notion of aimless eloquence began with the Sophists two thousand years ago:

> The sophists were the first to occupy themselves with a meditation upon words, their value, propriety, and function in the conduct of reasoning: the capital step toward *the discovery of style, conceived as a goal in itself, as an intrinsic end*, was taken [by the sophists].[9]

So, eloquence is a style of speaking or writing that is intrinsically pleasing without any reference to other aims. It has no aim. It's gratuitous. That's what makes it eloquent. If it had an aim, it would be rhetoric and would stand in the service of some cause or ideology.

An Enamored Reviewer

What aggravated me about the review of Donoghue's book in *Books and Culture* was that the Christian reviewer was so enamored by this view of eloquence that he thought all thinking evangelicals should read the book. Donoghue himself thought that the Bible—and Jesus, in particular—put significant obstacles in the way of seeing eloquence as aimless, gratuitous, pleasing language.[10] But the reviewer, on the contrary, was effusive about how this view shed light on the way God lavishes the world with superfluous, gratuitous eloquence:

> Is it really so hard to make the case for eloquence on Christian terms? What could be more eloquent, more blessedly superfluous, than Creation itself? All those beetles, those unseen creatures of the deep, those galaxies upon galaxies—all unnecessary. Shakespeare was unnecessary. My new grandson Gus is unnecessary.[11]

I don't think so. This is too cavalier about the purposefulness of God. Did God create this little boy Gus, and Shakespeare, and the galaxies, and the thousands of species of plants and animals we have yet to discover—did God create them whimsically or purposefully? If purposefully, they are not gratuitous. And they are not superfluous.

Not Deep Enough

The problem with Donoghue and his reviewer is that they haven't gone deep enough into the implications for eloquence of the existence of a God who governs all things and does all things *purposefully*— indeed, with the purpose to magnify the glory of his Son. "All things were created through him and for him" (Col. 1:16). Galaxies and grandsons are not gratuitous or superfluous. They are created for the glory of Jesus Christ. Even the galaxies we have not yet seen will serve to magnify the greatness of Christ.

So what shall we make of all these varied witnesses to the goodness of eloquence when, in view of Paul's statement in 1 Corinthians 1:17, "Christ did not send me to baptize but to preach the gospel, and *not with words of eloquent wisdom*, lest the cross of Christ be emptied of its power"? And what of 1 Corinthians 2:1, "I, when I came to you, brothers, did not come proclaiming to you the testimony of God *with lofty speech or wisdom*"?

The Sophist Connection

There is an interesting link between Donoghue's reference to the Sophists and the context of Paul's words to the Corinthians. Donoghue traces his view of eloquence back to the Sophists. They were the first to treat style "as a goal in itself, as an intrinsic end." One of the most compelling books on the background of Paul's words about eloquence in 1 Corinthians is Bruce Winter's *Philo and Paul among the Sophists*. Winter's argument is that it is precisely the Sophists and their view of eloquence that form the backdrop of what Paul says about his own speech and how he ministered in Corinth.[12]

So consider with me Paul's words in 1 Corinthians to see if he gives us enough clues to show what sort of eloquence he is rejecting and what sort he is not only not rejecting but using.[13]

Clues from 1 Corinthians

Notice in 1 Corinthians 1:10–12 that the Corinthian believers were forming divisions by lining up behind their favorite teachers, and there is pretty good evidence that the divisions had to do with the kind of eloquence the teachers had. It says in verse 12, "What I mean is that each one of you says, 'I follow Paul,' or 'I follow Apollos,' or 'I follow Cephas,' or 'I follow Christ.'"

We know from 2 Corinthians 10:10 that Paul's opponents mocked him as lacking eloquence. They said, "His letters are weighty and strong, but his bodily presence is weak, and *his speech of no account* [Gk. *ho logos exouthenemenos*]." And we know that Apollos, one of the favorites at Corinth, *was* eloquent because Acts 18:24 says, "Now a Jew named Apollos, a native of Alexandria, came to Ephesus. He was an eloquent man, competent in the Scriptures." The fact that he is from Alexandria is significant. Philo worked in Alexandria and tells us how prominent their Sophists were in training people to be eloquent.[14]

Opposing the Sophists

We know from at least six sources that the Sophists were also present in Corinth.[15] They put a huge premium on style and form as evidence of education and power and wisdom. They had probably influenced some in the church to admire their kind of eloquence and look for it in Christian teachers. Apollos probably became their celebrity because he was so good with words. Bruce Winter says, "Paul deliberately adopts an anti-sophistic stance and thus defends his church-planting activities in Corinth against a backdrop of sophistic conventions, perceptions and categories."[16]

That's what we find in 1 Corinthians 1:17, which is where we began this chapter: "Christ did not send me to baptize but to preach the gospel, and *not with words of eloquent wisdom*, lest the cross of Christ be emptied of its power." So the way Paul is going to oppose the eloquence of the Sophists is to show that it empties the cross. Why is that? Why does this view of eloquence empty the cross of power?

Undercutting Pride and Exalting Christ

Verse 18 gives part of the reason: "For the word of the cross is folly to those who are perishing, but to us who are being saved it is the power of God." The reason the cross can't fit in with the eloquence of the Sophists is that it is folly to them—that is, it is so destructive of human pride that those who aim at human praise through "rhetorically elaborated eloquence"[17] and "an elitist educational system"[18] could only see the cross as foolishness. The cross is the place where our sin is seen as most horrible and God's free grace shines most brightly. Both of these mean we deserve nothing. Therefore, the cross undercuts pride and exalts Christ, not us, and that made it foolish to the Sophists.

We see this confirmed in verse 20: "Where is the one who is wise? Where is the scribe? Where is the debater of this age?"—the debater, the man who is so nimble with his tongue that he can take either side and win. He is smooth and clever and verbally agile. Truth and content are not the issue; rhetorical maneuvering is. Paul says at the end of verse 20, "Has not God made foolish the wisdom of the world?" The wisdom in view is not any deep worldview over against Christianity; it's the sophistry of using language to win debates and show oneself clever and eloquent and powerful.

So the eloquence Paul is rejecting is not so much any particular language conventions but the exploitation of language to exalt self and belittle or ignore the crucified Lord. Notice the contrast again in chapter 2, verses 1–2: "And I, when I came to you, brothers, did not come proclaiming to you the testimony of God with lofty speech or wisdom. For I decided to know nothing among you except Jesus Christ and him crucified." The point is that wherever I meet scribes and debaters who bolster their ego with language jousting and leave the cross in the shadows, I am going to bring it out of the shadows and showcase it totally. I will refuse to play their language games.

A Two-pronged Criterion for Judging Eloquence

Notice one more thing in this context that gives us the two-pronged criterion of good and bad eloquence. In 1 Corinthians 1:26–29, Paul turns the tables on the Sophists' love affair with boasting.[19]

> For consider your calling, brothers: not many of you were wise according to worldly standards, not many were powerful, not many were of noble birth. But God chose what is foolish in the world to shame the wise; God chose what is weak in the world to shame the strong; God chose what is low and despised in the world, even things that are not, to bring to nothing things that are, so that no human being might boast in the presence of God.

Self-humiliation

God's design both in the cross and in election is "that no human being might boast in the presence of God." That is the first prong of our criterion of good and bad eloquence: *Does it feed boasting? Does it come from an ego in search of exaltation through clever speech?* If so, Paul rejects it.

Christ-exaltation

Then he continues in verses 30–31:

> And because of him you are in Christ Jesus, who became to us wisdom from God, righteousness and sanctification and redemption, so that, as it is written, "Let the one who boasts, boast in the Lord."

The second design of God, not only in the cross and in election but also in the sovereign grace of regeneration (v. 30, *"Because of him* you are in Christ Jesus"), is that all boasting be boasting in the Lord Jesus—the one who was crucified and raised. "Let the one who boasts, boast in the Lord." So the second prong of our criterion of good and bad eloquence is: *does it exalt Christ—especially the crucified Christ?*

Let me set out my understanding of Paul's two denunciations of eloquence. In 1 Corinthians 1:17 he says, ". . . *not with words of eloquent wisdom,* lest the cross of Christ be emptied of its power." And in 1 Corinthians 2:1–2 he says, ". . . [not] *with lofty speech or wisdom.* For I decided to know nothing among you except Jesus Christ and him crucified." The point of both is this: pride-sustaining, self-exalting use of words for a show of human wisdom is incompatible with finding your life and your glory in the cross of Christ. So let your use of words be governed by this double criterion: self-humiliation and Christ-exaltation.

If we put these two criteria in front of all our efforts to make an impact through word selection and word arrangement and word delivery—that is, if we put them in front of our attempts at eloquence—I think we will be guarded from the misuse of eloquence that Paul rejected. And now I see more clearly that behind James Denney's dictum is precisely these two criteria: "No man can give the impression that he himself is clever and that Christ is mighty to save." Self-exaltation and Christ-exaltation can't go together.

The Bible Is Eloquent
So when we go back to Calvin and Luther and John Donne—all of whom said that the Bible is filled with eloquence—I conclude they are right. The Bible is filled with every manner of literary device to add impact to the language: acrostics, alliteration, analogy, anthropomorphism, assonance, cadence, chiasm, consonance, dialogue, hyperbole, irony, metaphor, meter, onomatopoeia, paradox, parallelism, repetition, rhyme, satire, simile—they're all there, and more.

And it seems to me that God invites us to join him in this creativity of eloquence. He beckons us with words like:

> To make an apt answer is a joy to a man,
>   and a word in season, how good it is! (Prov. 15:23)

> A word fitly spoken
>   is like apples of gold in a setting of silver. (Prov. 25:11)[20]

> Like a lame man's legs, which hang useless,
>> is a proverb in the mouth of fools. (Prov. 26:7)

> And whatever you do, in *word* or deed, do everything in the name of the Lord Jesus, giving thanks to God the Father through him. (Col. 3:17)

In other words, give thought to the aptness and seasonableness and fitness and timing and appropriateness of your words. And make all of them an honor to the name of the Lord Jesus.

What Difference Does It Make?

There is one last question I want to take up. If we are permitted to pursue eloquence (powerful verbal impact) indeed, if we are invited to, and if the Bible is an abundantly eloquent book, and if we are guided in our pursuit of this impact by the double criterion of self-humiliation and Christ-exaltation—what would be our hope for our speech or writing if we succeeded? Since only the Holy Spirit can perform the miracle of new birth and actually raise the spiritually dead, and since he can do it with mundane, pedestrian witnesses to the gospel or eloquent witnesses to the gospel, what difference does it make if we strive for any measure of eloquence or increased impact through language?

Five Hopes in Christian Eloquence

Here is a starter list of five things that we may hope for, knowing that anywhere along the way, God may step in and make our words instruments of salvation, with or without eloquence.

1) Keeping Interest

Artistic, surprising, provocative, or aesthetically pleasing language choices (that is, eloquence) may keep people awake and focused because they find it interesting or unusual or pleasing for reasons they cannot articulate. When the disciples fell asleep in Gethsemane, Jesus said, "The spirit indeed is willing, but the flesh is weak" (Matt. 26:41). We need to help people's weaknesses.

This is not conversion or even conviction or sanctification, but it is a serious means to those ends. Sleeping people or distracted people do not hear the Word, and faith comes by hearing and hearing by the Word. Therefore, eloquence is like a good night's sleep. It won't save your soul, but it might keep you awake to hear the Word, which can save your soul. So a person's style may keep you interested and awake to the same end.

2) Gaining Sympathy

Artistic, surprising, provocative, or aesthetically pleasing language may bring an adversarial mind into greater sympathy with the speaker. If the language is interesting and fresh enough, obstacles may be overcome—boredom, anger, resentment, suspicion—and replaced with respect and attraction and interest and concentration. These are not conversion or conviction or sanctification, but they don't drive a person farther away like boredom does. They may in fact draw a person so close to the light that Jesus says, "You are not far from the kingdom of God" (Mark 12:34).

For example, return to George Whitefield and Benjamin Franklin for a moment. Whitefield's eloquence overwhelmed Franklin. He did not think Whitefield was a sham. He admired him. He became one of Whitefield's closest friends. Whitefield biographer Harry Stout says, "Franklin allowed himself to be drawn out on the subject of personal religiosity with Whitefield as with no one else, finding in Whitefield a listener he could trust—if not agree with."[21] Therefore, Whitefield could speak to Franklin about Christ as no one else could. He explained to Franklin with a smile: "I must have something of Christ in all my letters."[22] Who knows how close Whitefield came to winning Franklin to the faith—and all this because Whitefield's eloquence overcame Franklin's disdain for the Revival.

3) Awakening Sensitivity

Fresh, surprising, provocative, aesthetically pleasing speech may have an awakening effect on a person's mind and heart that is short of regeneration but still important as an awakening of emotional and intellectual sensitivity for more serious and beautiful things. If a poetic turn of phrase can cause people to notice the magnificence of the sun, their next step might be to see that the heavens are telling the glory of God (Ps. 19:1), and then they might confess Christ as the great sun of righteousness (Mal. 4:2).

Is that not why David, the great poet of Israel, first says, "The heavens declare the glory of God" (Ps. 19:1), and then says, "In them he has set a tent for the sun, which comes out like a bridegroom leaving his chamber, and, like a strong man, runs its course with joy" (Ps.19:4–5)? Why compare the rising sun to a bridegroom and a runner? To help the dull mind awaken to the joyful beauty of the rising sun in the hopes that this natural kind of awakening might lead to the spiritual sight that nature is all about the glory of God.

4) Speaking Memorably

Certain kinds of eloquence—cadence, parallelism, meter, rhyme, assonance, consonance—may not only interest and awaken the heart but increase that impact by making what is said memorable, that is, more easy to remember or memorize. Consider the title of this book. I am very picky when it comes to cadence and consonance and assonance. I worked on the title—*The Power of Words and the Wonder of God*—the same way I work on a poem. I want it to be pleasing and memorable.

- First, there is an intentional *cadence* or meter that I find pleasing: ("The POWer of WORDS and the WONder of GOD").
- Second, there is *consonance* or alliteration between the W's in "Words" and "Wonder." Compare "The Power of Language and the Wonder of God" or "The Power of Words and the Majesty of God." Both cadence and alliteration are lost.
- Third, there is assonance. Six of the nine words are dominated by the sound of the letter O: "Power," "of," "Words," "Wonder," "of," "God." Compare: "The Strength of Language and the Marvel of Deity."
- Finally, I think the juxtaposition of "Words" and "Wonder" and "God" is unusual, provocative, and attractive.

All of that, I think, helps people remember the title, not because it is displeasing—the way 9/11 is remembered because it hurt—but because it is aesthetically satisfying.

I assume that this mnemonic purpose is why some parts of the Bible are written in acrostics. For example, Psalm 119 is 22 stanzas of 8 verses each, and each stanza begins with a different letter of the Hebrew alphabet, and all 8 verses in each stanza begin with that letter. That is not careless but intentional, artistic, eloquent.

5) Increasing Power

The attempt to craft striking and beautiful language makes it possible that the beauty of eloquence can join with the beauty of truth and increase the power of your words. When we take care to create a beautiful way of speaking or writing about something beautiful, the eloquence—the beauty of the form—reflects and honors the beauty of the subject and so honors the truth.

The method and the matter become one, and the totality of both becomes a witness to the truth and beauty of the message. If the glory of Christ is always ultimately our subject, and if he created all things, and if he upholds all things, then bringing the beauty of form into harmony with the beauty of truth is the fullest way to honor the Lord.

Or another way to think about this unity is this: if people see and delight in the beauty of your language but do not yet see the beauty of the Lord Jesus, you have given them not only a witness to his beauty but an invitation. You have said, "It's like this, only better. The beauty of my words is the shadow. Christ, who created and sustains and mercifully accepts imperfect beauty, is the substance. Turn to him. Go to him."

Creating Eloquence for His Name's Sake

Yes, there is Christian eloquence. It is not the decisive factor in salvation or sanctification; God is. But faith comes by hearing, and hearing by the Word. That word in the Bible is pervasively eloquent—words are put together in a way to give great impact. And God invites us to create our own eloquent phrases for his name's sake, not ours. And in the mystery of his sovereign grace, he will glorify himself in the hearts of others in spite of and because of the words we have chosen. In that way, he will keep us humble and get all the glory for himself. Amen.

CHAPTER FOUR

How Sharp the Edge? Christ, Controversy, and Cutting Words

Mark Driscoll

WORDS. Our God works through words.

The words of Scripture reveal that the world we live in sprang into existence by the Word of God. With majestic words Psalm 33:6 preaches, "By the word of the LORD the heavens were made, and by the breath of his mouth all their host."

When God chose to enter into the world he had made, he did so by revealing Jesus Christ as no less than the Word of God. With history-shattering words John 1:14 thunders, "And the Word became flesh and dwelt among us, and we have seen his glory, glory as of the only Son from the Father, full of grace and truth."

Throughout God's Word, the Scriptures, God speaks tough and tender words to his people. He curses and he blesses. His words kill and his words give life. He speaks law from Mount Sinai and he speaks gospel from Golgotha. This balance between tough and tender speech is rooted ultimately in the character of God himself. Subsequently, Paul calls the church at Rome to consider both the kindness and the severity of God (Rom. 11:22). Tender words and tough words, spoken in love, fill the pages of the Bible. These words are a gracious gift because they reveal to us the fullness of God so that our speech may echo his. In order to inform and transform our words, we will examine the Word of God to hear his tender and tough words to sheep, swine, wolves, dogs, and shepherds.

Feed the Sheep

Sheep are the most frequently mentioned animal in all of Scripture. Ezekiel 34 is arguably the most comprehensive section in all of Scripture on sheep, false shepherds, true shepherds, and God as the Shepherd. Sheep are consistently portrayed there in less than powerful and awe-inspiring depiction. Sheep are prone to wander because they are foolish. Sheep are prone to follow false shepherds and be led astray because they are not discerning. Sheep are prone to get pushed around, leaving them hungry, thirsty, and weary. Sheep are so defenseless that they are commonly wounded and killed without even putting up a fight. The Bible is clear that Christians are sheep.

So when the Bible commands pastors to "shepherd the flock" (1 Pet. 5:1–3), the expectation is that loving, patient, kind, devoted, and humble shepherds will give their lives to care for their flock like Jesus Christ the "good shepherd" (John 10:11, 14). The Gospels continually report how Jesus shepherded with loving honesty and gracious empathy. In John 4 he sat down at a well with a perverted, outcast Samaritan woman to care for her when no one else would. Similarly, Paul demonstrates the tender care of a good shepherd throughout his ministry, including when he graciously accommodated the tender consciences of Christian vegetarians (Romans 14).

Perhaps the most succinct directive about words for sheep is found in Ephesians 4:29–32:

> Let no corrupting talk come out of your mouths, but only such as is good for building up, as fits the occasion, that it may give grace to those who hear. And do not grieve the Holy Spirit of God, by whom you were sealed for the day of redemption. Let all bitterness and wrath and anger and clamor and slander be put away from you, along with all malice. Be kind to *one another*, tenderhearted, forgiving *one another*, as God in Christ forgave you.

This section of Scripture is incredibly important because it reveals how sheep are to speak to other sheep and how shepherds are to speak to sheep, including tone and content. Paul's phrase "one another" reveals that; however, there are Christians who would make these the defining marks of all true godly speech. Besides sheep, the Bible also speaks of swine, wolves, and dogs. Thus, any attempt to require that every Christian speak to everyone as if all are a sheep is unbiblical. Why? Because not everyone is a sheep.

Rebuke the Swine

In Bible times, swine were dirty animals that often roamed the street scavenging for food. Pigs were also "unclean" for God's people. Not surprisingly, *swine* became a derogatory word in the culture for people who claimed to worship God but lived a hypocritical life of filthy, unrepentant sin. This explains why the prodigal son ended up eating with the pigs after living in habitual sin (Luke 15:11–32), why Jesus said we should not give pearls to pigs (Matt. 7:6), and why the woman in Proverbs 11:22 is called a pig: "Like a gold ring in a pig's snout is a beautiful woman without discretion."

Simply, the Bible teaches and models the need for us to rebuke the swine. However, as soon as swine start getting mocked, they invariably huddle together and squeal about how their feelings were hurt because shepherds criticized their alternative mud lifestyle. Subsequently, a few well-intended but less-than-wise sheep invariably take up their offense and accuse the shepherds of not being loving. These sheep quote Bible verses about love out of context while overlooking all the verses about rebuke.

One example is when Paul exhorts Timothy: "As for those who persist in sin, rebuke them in the presence of all" (1 Tim. 5:20). Paul also says, "Preach the word; be ready in season and out of season; reprove, rebuke, and exhort" (2 Tim. 4:2). Another example is when Paul commands Titus "to give instruction in sound doctrine and also to rebuke those who contradict it" (Titus 1:9), "rebuke them sharply" (Titus 1:13), and "exhort and rebuke with all authority" (Titus 2:15).

Worldliness occurs when we take the ways of godless people and impose them on God's people, as if those ways were God's ways. Sometimes worldliness is blazingly obvious, like when a pastor denies that people need Jesus for salvation because he took some classes at the local community college and learned big words that end with -ism (e.g., postmodernism, antifoundationalism, perspectivism). Other times, worldliness is far subtler, like when people who claim to worship a God who was murdered, in part for his tough words, judge

Christian speech by Victorian politeness, politically correct tolerance, or just plain yellow-bellied Midwestern nicety.

One of the great themes of the Protestant Reformation was that Scripture—not culture—is best suited to interpret Scripture. If at any point our cultural preferences are in contradiction to Scripture, it is culture that must move and not Scripture.

In order to understand what the Bible means when it exhorts us to rebuke the swine, we will spend some considerable time simply reading what God's Word actually says to swine. As you read, imagine the texts being thundered from the pulpit of your local church, declared in the stump speech of a politician running for office, portrayed in the media campaign of a major corporation, or simply read on your nightly news by a guy who does not wince or apologize—that is how forceful these texts were in their original contexts.

Isaiah tells the most seductive saints with low-cut blouses and high-cut skirts:

> The LORD said:
> Because the daughters of Zion are haughty
>   and walk with outstretched necks,
>   glancing wantonly with their eyes,
> mincing along as they go,
>   tinkling with their feet,
> therefore the Lord will strike with a scab
>   the heads of the daughters of Zion,
>   and the LORD will lay bare their secret parts. (Isa. 3:16–17)

In that day the Lord will take away the finery of the anklets, the headbands, and the crescents; the pendants, the bracelets, and the scarves; the headdresses, the armlets, the sashes, the perfume boxes, and the amulets; the signet rings and nose rings; the festal robes, the mantles, the cloaks, and the handbags; the mirrors, the linen garments, the turbans, and the veils.

> Instead of perfume there will be rottenness;
>   and instead of a belt, a rope;
> and instead of well-set hair, baldness;
>   and instead of a rich robe, a skirt of sackcloth;
>   and branding instead of beauty. (Isa. 3:24)

Virtually the entire book of Amos is a rebuke to swine. The painfully devastating satire is pointed at rich women who are fat cows and get drunk at concerts and act like Paris Hilton's BFF. God's word to wealthy women in Amos 4:1 is, "Hear this word, you cows of Bashan, who are on the mountain of Samaria, who oppress the poor, who crush the needy, who say to your husbands, 'Bring, that we may drink!'" God's word in Amos 6:4–6 is, "Woe to those who lie on beds of ivory and stretch themselves out on their couches, and eat lambs from the flock and calves from the midst of the stall, who sing idle songs to the sound of the harp and like David invent for themselves instruments of music, who drink wine in bowls and anoint themselves with the finest oils."

Sometimes, God's rebuke is incredibly graphic. This is because bad things (like whoring) need bad words (like *whoring*) and not good words (like *partner*); otherwise people get confused, especially dumb sheep. Perhaps the most graphic words of God are found in Ezekiel. In Ezekiel 16:25–27 God says:

> At the head of every street you built your lofty place and made your beauty an abomination, offering yourself to any passerby and multiplying your whoring. You also played the whore with the Egyptians, your lustful neighbors, multiplying your whoring, to provoke me to anger. Behold, therefore, I stretched out my hand against you and diminished your allotted portion and delivered you to the greed of your enemies, the daughters of the Philistines, who were ashamed of your lewd behavior.

Also, in Ezekiel 23:18–21 (NIV) God says:

> When she carried on her prostitution openly and exposed her nakedness, I turned away from her in disgust, just as I had turned away from her sister. Yet she became more and more promiscuous as she recalled the days of her youth, when she was a prostitute in Egypt. There she lusted after her lovers, whose genitals were like those of donkeys and whose emission was like that of horses. So you longed for the lewdness of your youth, when in Egypt your bosom was caressed and your young breasts fondled.

Proverbs is littered with similar rebukes to swine. Scattered throughout the book are repeated rebukes of loud women, whoring women, foolish women, nagging women, and contentious women. Some of the best rebukes are reserved for women who are impossible to live with. Their husbands are encouraged to haul their hunting gear out of the garage, drag it onto the roof, and camp on the house rather than live in it. Otherwise they might end up with a gun in their mouth, reading Lamentations before they die as a way to get out of marriage without grounds for divorce.

Proverbs also rebukes swinish men for being greedy, perverted, foolish, proud, and disorganized. Such men are often called sluggards. They are mocked for making dumb excuses for their lazy lifestyle (e.g., Prov. 22:13), and for being too lazy to even make the effort to get a slice of delivered pizza from the box to their mouth (e.g., Prov. 19:24). The repeated digs at sluggards throughout Proverbs are hilarious—unless of course you are an able-bodied guy in his thirties who still lives with his mom because she cuts his sandwiches into little-boy squares before tucking him in for nappies between his Tigger and Roo sheets. These poor guys often wear themselves out blogging and playing in fantasy sports leagues.

Admittedly, fat-cow, high-maintenance wives, half-naked young women whom God shaved like boot camp recruits, and men hung like donkeys with semen like fire hoses do not make the flannel graphs for kids at the local Baptist church for good reason. Still, they did make the Bible and thus should find a place in our theology of words. Why? Because they are rare but necessary examples of how to rebuke the swine. If we really love the swine, we need to use tough words to ensure they understand how filthy they are so they can bathe in repentance. Indeed, as 2 Timothy 3:16 (NIV) says, "*All* Scripture is God-breathed and is useful for . . . rebuking."

We will now study more of God's Word to learn the long-lost skill of biblical wolf hunting.

Shoot the Wolves

Wolves are heretics, false teachers, and, generally speaking, anyone who ravages the flock and feasts on the sheep. In addition to calling them wolves (Ezek. 22:27; Zeph. 3:3; Matt. 7:15; 10:16; Luke 10:3; Acts 20:29), the Bible also calls them dogs and evildoers (Phil. 3:2), empty and deceitful (Col. 2:8), puffed up without reason (Col. 2:18), given to mythical speculation and vanity without understanding

(1 Tim. 1:3–7), products of a shipwrecked faith (1 Tim. 1:19), demonic liars with a seared conscience (1 Tim. 4:1–2), peddlers of silly myths (1 Tim. 4:7), arrogant fools with depraved minds (1 Tim. 6:3–5), the spiritual equivalent of gangrene (2 Tim. 2:14–18), foolish and ignorant (2 Tim. 2:23), chatty deceivers (Titus 1:10–14), destructive blasphemers (2 Pet. 2:1–3), ignorantly unstable (2 Pet. 3:16), and antichrists (1 John 2:18). The Bible does not call wolves best-selling authors, bishops, or pastors, though they also commonly prefer to use those names on their business cards.

The Bible is clear that we are not to treat wolves in the same way that we treat sheep. The great Protestant Reformer Martin Luther said it well: "With the wolves you cannot be too severe; with the weak sheep you cannot be too gentle."[1] Luther also said,

> A preacher must not only feed the sheep so as to instruct them how they are to be good Christians, but he must also keep the wolves from attacking the sheep and leading them astray with false doctrine and error, for the devil is never idle. Nowadays there are many people who are quite ready to tolerate our preaching of the Gospel as long as we do not cry out against the wolves and preach against the prelates. But though I preach the truth, feed the sheep well, and give them good instruction, this is still not enough unless the sheep are also guarded and protected so that the wolves do not come and carry them off.[2]

Likewise, Pastor Douglas Wilson has said:

> Sheep are to be kind to sheep. Shepherds are to be kind to sheep. But if a shepherd is kind to wolves, that is just another way to let them savage the sheep. Kindness to sheep is hostility to wolves. Kindness to wolves is hostility to sheep. All attempts to get the wolves and sheep together for some kind of an ecumenical lovefest will only result in fat, contented wolves.[3]

Jesus himself was known to shoot the wolves. He sends the most bullets flying in Matthew 23—the equivalent of a gunfight between him and some of the most devoutly religious people in his day. They started off fighting for the Bible but wound up fighting for religious ideas not founded on the Bible. Commenting on Matthew 23, D. A. Carson says:

Jesus now goes on the offensive, and "offensive" is not too strong a word for much of the language he uses. . . . It shows Jesus as a fierce controversialist, quite willing to make enemies when the cause demanded it. The target was the scribes (*teachers of the law*, a class of professional interpreters of Scriptures and of rabbinic tradition), and *the Pharisees*, a religious "party" to which most scribes belonged, and which was devoted to scrupulous observance of the full range of rabbinic legislation. They were, generally speaking, earnest, moral people, and Jesus' attack here seems to many harsh and unfair. But his concern was not so much with their performance as individuals, but with the system of religious observance which they upheld. In insisting on a huge and growing corpus of rules and regulations, they were in danger of ignoring inner attitudes and motives and of putting adherence to the system before the will of God.[4]

Standing in line with the Old Testament prophets, in Matthew 23 Jesus pronounces seven woes on the wolves. The language of "woe" was a public, passionate declaration, with some of the guilty present for his proclamation of displeasure, grief, judgment, and righteous anger. Jesus' words are a devastating series of shots at the wolves in front of the sheep:

They preach, but do not practice. They tie up heavy burdens, hard to bear, and lay them on people's shoulders, but they themselves are not willing to move them with their finger. They do all their deeds to be seen by others . . . and they love the place of honor at feasts and the best seats in the synagogues and greetings in the marketplaces and being called rabbi by others. . . .

But woe to you, scribes and Pharisees, hypocrites! For you shut the kingdom of heaven in people's faces. For you neither enter yourselves nor allow those who would enter to go in. Woe to you, scribes and Pharisees, hypocrites! For you travel across sea and land to make a single proselyte, and when he becomes a proselyte, you make him twice as much a child of hell as yourselves.

Woe to you, blind guides. . . . You blind fools! . . . You blind men! . . .

Woe to you, scribes and Pharisees, hypocrites! For you tithe mint and dill and cumin, and have neglected the weightier matters of the law: justice and mercy and faithfulness. These you ought to have done, without neglecting the others. You blind guides, straining out a gnat and swallowing a camel!

> Woe to you, scribes and Pharisees, hypocrites! For you clean the outside of the cup and the plate, but inside they are full of greed and self-indulgence.
>
> You blind Pharisee! . . .
>
> Woe to you, scribes and Pharisees, hypocrites! For you are like whitewashed tombs, which outwardly appear beautiful, but within are full of dead people's bones and all uncleanness. So you also outwardly appear righteous to others, but within you are full of hypocrisy and lawlessness.
>
> Woe to you, scribes and Pharisees, hypocrites! For you build the tombs of the prophets and decorate the monuments of the righteous, saying, "If we had lived in the days of our fathers, we would not have taken part with them in shedding the blood of the prophets." Thus you witness against yourselves that you are sons of those who murdered the prophets. Fill up, then, the measure of your fathers. You serpents, you brood of vipers, how are you to escape being sentenced to hell? (Matt. 23:3–33)

This harsh language was undoubtedly very shocking to a bunch of guys who went to seminary and read big books, including the footnotes. They had really prayed about it and did not agree that their inner child needed a spanking, and nearly all the comments on their blog were on their side, saying that Jesus needed to take some meds and meet with Dr. Phil.

When he shoots the wolves, a shepherd is not only protecting the sheep but also evangelizing non-Christians. In fact, many churches that love the Bible and are doctrinally sound but lack converts would be well served by learning how to shoot the wolves like Jesus does in Matthew 23. There Jesus shot the wolves publically in front of a crowd. In that crowd would have been an assortment of wolves, sheep, and lost people. By calling the religious people to repent of their proud, hypocritical, unbiblical, unloving, legalistic, and self-righteous religion, he was demonstrating the fact that God, as Paul says in Acts 17:30, "commands all people everywhere to repent." For repentance to occur, sinners must be called to repent of their sins, and religious people need to be called to repent of their religion.

Sadly, most gospel preaching is only half true because it calls only the "sinners" to repent of their sin. Subsequently, fornicators, adulterers, perverts, liars, thieves, and the like are called to repent of their sin.

This is quite good. However, what is often lacking in gospel preaching is an equally passionate call for the smug holier-than-thou religious types to get off their high horse (Jesus called it "Moses' seat" in Matthew 23) and repent of their religion that is simply another kind of sin.

When the example of Jesus in Matthew 23 is not followed, the result is that sinners just think Christians are mean-spirited, self-righteous, religious prigs who want them to become religious too; thus, these non-Christians are as interested in Jesus as a cat is in water. The smug religious types cheer on the preaching-to-the-choir preachers who lather the wolves into a frenzy, shouting about how the wicked people outside their church are kindling for the flames of hell. True gospel preaching will not divide people into sinners and righteous, but rather into repentant and unrepentant, with both unrepentant sinners and religious wolves wanting to silence the shepherd and ravage his repentant flock.

We see wolves being shot elsewhere in the New Testament. Paul admonished the Judaizers in Galatia, who thought they were holy because they were circumcised a bit, to go Lorena Bobbitt and cut the whole thing off. This literally would have meant that these wolves would no longer be accepted as Jews, and not only cut off physically but also cut off spiritually from temple worship. Nonetheless, Paul says:

> But if I, brothers, still preach circumcision, why am I still being persecuted? In that case the offense of the cross has been removed. I wish those who unsettle you would emasculate themselves! For you were called to freedom, brothers. Only do not use your freedom as an opportunity for the flesh, but through love serve one another. For the whole law is fulfilled in one word: "You shall love your neighbor as yourself." (Gal. 5:11–14)

How curious it is that sheep and wolves alike are prone to quote the latter half of this section of God's Word and argue that we should be loving, as Jesus taught, while conveniently ignoring the part about cutting oneself off. Indeed, when the Bible says we need to be loving, we need to read the verses around those words to see how the Bible also exemplifies how to be loving to God, sheep, lost people, and wolves. Apparently, in some cases telling religious wolves to emasculate themselves is loving.

Not only does the Word of God record the shooting of packs

of wolves, such as Pharisees and Judaizers, but it also names individual wolves to be shot. Paul says, "Some have made shipwreck of their faith, among whom are Hymenaeus and Alexander, whom I have handed over to Satan" (1 Tim. 1:19–20). Later he speaks of "Hymenaeus and Philetus, who have swerved from the truth" (2 Tim. 2:17–18) and how "Alexander the coppersmith did [him] great harm" (2 Tim. 4:14).

Outside of Scripture, one of the most legendary wolf hunters in the history of the church is Martin Luther. He was a good shot with bad papists. Gordon Rupp argues that, like the Old Testament prophets and Paul, Luther used colorful language in order to repulse readers and make them see how vile apostasy and sin really are. Rupp writes that, for Luther, "blasphemy and apostasy are not simply evil: they are filthy things, which must be described in language coarse enough and repulsive enough to nauseate the reader."[5]

Luther defended his usage of colorful and incisive speech as being both Christlike and apostolic. Luther writes:

> It is true, I have, by and large, sharply inveighed against ungodly doctrines and have not been slow to bite my adversaries, not because of their bad morals but because of their ungodliness. Of this I am so unrepentant that I have resolved to continue in this burning zeal and to despise the judgment of men, after the example of Christ, who in His zeal called His adversaries a generation of vipers, blind, hypocrites, children of the devil (Matt. 23:13; 17:33; John 8:44). And Paul calls the sorcerer a child of the devil full of all subtlety and all mischief (Acts 13:10); and some false apostles he calls dogs, deceivers, and adulterers of the Word (Phil. 3:2; 2 Cor. 11:13). If these sensitive ears had heard this, they would probably say that no one could be more biting and immoderate than Paul. Who is more biting than the prophets? But nowadays, of course, our ears are made so sensitive by the mad multitude of flatterers that as soon as we find that we are not praised in all things, we cry out that people are vicious; and when we cannot ward off the truth under any other guise, we escape from it under the pretext of the snappishness, impatience, and immoderateness of its defenders. What good does salt do if it does not bite? What good does the edge of the sword do if it does not cut? Cursed be the man who does the work of the Lord deceitfully![6]

Luther never denied that his polemics were vehement. Luther defended his colorful language by appealing to the fact that God's Word was being assailed. Luther continues:

> I cannot deny that I am more vehement than I should be. . . . But they assail me and God's Word so atrociously and criminally that were I not carried away to write warmly, even a mind of stone might be moved to war by indignation. How much more, then, would I, who have a warm temperament and a pen that is not at all blunt, be moved to war! These monsters are carrying me beyond the bounds of moderation. I wonder whence this new scrupulousness is born which calls all that is said against an opponent abuse. What do you think of Christ? Was He abusive when He called the Jews an adulterous and perverse generation, an offspring of vipers, hypocrites, and children of the devil? Paul, too, speaks of dogs, vain babblers, seducers, unlearned. In Acts 13:10 he rages against a false prophet in such a way that he might seem to be insane. He says: "O full of all guile and all villainy, thou son of the devil, thou enemy of all truth!" Why does he here not rather modestly flatter this fellow in order to convert him instead of thundering in such a way? The truth, which one is conscious of possessing, cannot be patient against its obstinate and intractable enemies.[7]

Luther reserved some of his strongest and most colorful language for his theological opponents. One such opponent was Erasmus of Rotterdam. Two entries from Luther's *Table Talk* make plain his feelings toward the man: "Erasmus of Rotterdam is the vilest miscreant that ever disgraced the earth. He made several attempts to draw me into his snares. . . . He is a very Caiaphas."[8] Luther also wrote:

> Erasmus is very pitiful with his prefaces, though he tries to smooth them over; he appears to see no difference between Jesus Christ our Savior, and the wise pagan legislator Solon. He sneers at St Paul and St John; and ventures to say, that the Epistle to the Romans, what ever it might have been at a former period, is not applicable to the present state of things. Shame upon thee, accursed wretch! 'Tis a mere Momus, making his mows and mocks at everything and everybody, at God and man, at papist and protestant, but all the while using such shuffling and double-meaning terms, that no one can lay hold of him to any effectual purpose. Whenever I pray, I pray for a curse upon Erasmus.[9]

For modern ears finely tuned to prefer only tender tones, the words of Luther are perhaps quickly dismissed as the rants of an angry man, as if all anger is bad and less civilized than herbal tea, deep-breathing exercises, and the lotus position. The truth is that sometimes Luther's public speech was fueled by intense anger. In his defense, Luther makes a distinction between speech that is fueled by self-righteous anger and speech that is fueled by righteous indignation. Luther believed that righteous anger often fueled his defense of the gospel, even saying, "I have no better remedy than anger. If I want to write, pray, preach well, then I must be angry. Then my entire blood supply refreshes itself, my mind is made keen, and all temptations depart."[10] It appears that while some people start their day with coffee Luther found it more effective to start the day with anger.

Indeed, some Christians are always angry and won't stop fighting. But it is equally true that some Christians are rarely angry and won't start fighting. The former are always renounced while the latter legion gets away with perennial cowardice in the name of nicety.

Some things are not worth fighting over, and many a church fight and strained relationship is evidence of the wisdom of Proverbs 19:11, which says, "Good sense makes one slow to anger, and it is his glory to overlook an offense." Conversely, Ecclesiastes 3:8 rightly says that there is also "a time to love, and a time to hate; a time for war, and a time for peace."

Discernment is knowing what time it is. Courage is doing what the time requires. While not every church needs a Martin Luther, more than a handful of denominations could use a good shooter, because the wolves have the sheep praying to the demon gods of other religions while encouraging the rams to have sex with the rams and the ewes to have sex with the ewes.

Beat the Dogs

Dogs are often loathed in the Bible because they were prone to wander wildly, eat anything (including human remains), and cause trouble, including terrifying people by chasing and barking at them. It is not surprising that the Old Testament refers to greedy spiritual leaders as dogs who are always looking for more and never have enough (Isa. 56:10–11); they encircle God's leaders to bark at them in intimidation, hoping to devour them (Ps. 22:16, 20). In the New Testament, Philippians 3:2 says, "Look out for the dogs, look out for the evildoers." Galatians 5:15 warns, "But if you bite and devour one another, watch out that you are not consumed by one another." In addition, Revelation 22:15 paints this image of heaven: "Outside are the dogs and sorcerers and the sexually immoral and murderers and idolaters, and everyone who loves and practices falsehood."

Dogs are those people who bark at God's people in an effort to control them, intimidate them, manipulate them, use them, abuse them, terrify them, harm them, and devour them. Their barks can be threats, demands, false teaching, relational manipulation, emotional control, pushiness, rudeness, and unfounded criticism.

A good pastoral shepherd must consider his responsibility to feed and defend the sheep when considering how to deal with the dogs. Thus, when the dogs encircle the flock, it is the shepherd's duty to take his staff in his hand and beat the dogs with great force until they yelp and flee in defeat. The staff in the shepherd's hand is often the stinging weapon of strong language, humor, irony, sarcasm, ridicule, and mockery. Regarding this mighty staff for the beating of the dogs, the renowned Reformed Baptist preacher Charles Haddon Spurgeon said, "The man who serves his God with his whole heart is apt to forget his surroundings, and to fling himself so completely into his work that the whole of his nature comes into action, and even his humor, if he be possessed of that faculty, rushes into the battle."[11] Spurgeon also said, "I do not know why ridicule is to be given up to Satan as a weapon to be used against us, and not to be employed by us as a weapon against him.[12]

Elsewhere, Spurgeon mentions Martin Luther's devastating use of humor to beat some dogs in his day. Church historian Roland H. Bainton writes:

> Luther delighted less in muck than many of the literary men of his age; but if he did indulge, he excelled in this as in every other area of speech. The volume of coarseness, in his total output is slight. Detractors have sifted from the pitchblende of his ninety tomes a few pages of radioactive vulgarity.[13]

Some of Luther's sharpest blows were reserved for dogs who refused to argue from Scripture. Luther lost patience with those who could not show him from the Bible that he was wrong. Luther writes: "How often must I cry out to you coarse, stupid papists to quote Scripture sometime? Scripture! Scripture! Scripture! Do you not hear, you deaf goat and coarse ass?"[14] Luther argued that his theological opponents avoided the Bible: "I cry: Gospel, Gospel, Gospel! Christ, Christ! Then they reply: The fathers! The fathers! Custom, Custom! Statutes, Statutes! But when I say: The fathers, custom, and the statutes have often been in error; matters of this kind must be settled by a stronger and more reliable authority; but Christ cannot be in error—then they are more speechless than fish."[15] Reflecting on one of his many debates with a Roman Catholic scholar who refused to appeal to Scripture, Luther writes:

> I demand Scripture from him; then he answers me with sayings of the teachers. I ask for the sun; then he shows me his lantern. I ask: Where is the Scripture? Then he says: Step forward, Ambrosius; step forward, Cyril; and the like. See there! Is this not the game of the builders at Babylon (Gen. 11:7) who bring wood when one calls for water and yet shout as though they had filled the order very well? Tell me, who can fear such blockheads?[16]

The problem with dogs is that their bark is worse than their bite, and if the sheep take them seriously they will suffer. So, the best thing a good shepherd can do is beat the dogs with mockery, revealing them to be merely fangless, clawless liars with nothing more than a bark to fear.

Before examining instances of controversial and comedic biblical beatings, it would be helpful to understand the importance of satire as a literary device in the Bible. The *Dictionary of Biblical Imagery* says,

> Satire is the exposure of human vice or folly through rebuke or ridicule. . . . It might consist of an entire book (e.g., Amos), or it can be as small as an individual proverb. One of the conventions of satire is the freedom to exaggerate, overstate or oversimplify to make a satiric point. Overall, satire is a subversive form that questions the status quo, unsettles people's thinking, assaults the deep structure of conventional thought patterns and aims to make people uncomfortable. . . .

> Horatian satire (named after Horace) is light, urbane and subtle. It uses a low-pressure approach in attempting to influence an audience toward a negative assessment of the thing being attacked. . . . Juvenalian satire (named after Juvenal) is biting, bitter and angry. . . . We might say that one approach attempts to *laugh* vice or folly out of existence, and the other to *lash* it out of existence.[17]

Psalm 1 exhorts us to not sit with those who mock everyone, and to not to scoff God because no one is to mock God. However, God gets to mock a lot of people who take themselves too seriously and him too lightly, thereby needing to be taken down a few pegs for their good and his glory (Pss. 2:4; 59:8; Prov. 1:26). Indeed, anyone with even a modicum of humor and an eye for the details readily sees some very funny satirical mockery littered throughout the pages of Scripture.

First Kings 18 records the legendary octagon showdown between Elijah and the prophets of Baal. When their god failed to show up, "Elijah mocked them, saying, 'Cry aloud, for he is a god. Either he is musing, or he is relieving himself, or he is on a journey, or perhaps he is asleep and must be awakened'" (1 Kings 18:27). Commenting on this text, Doug Wilson says, "The passage is plain—Elijah mocked them. And in the original Hebrew he is even more pointed. Perhaps your god is off in the bathroom. His prophets are all gathered in the hallway with an anxious look on their faces. Bang on the door louder. He's been in there a long time."[18] Martin Luther actually justified his mocking tone by appealing to the Old Testament prophets: "I trust that I am justified in mocking those who mock my God and His Word and work. Elijah, too, mocked the prophets of Baal (1 Kings 18:27)."[19]

Isaiah 44:15–17 sounds like a Monty Python sketch of a guy who chops down a tree and then

> takes a part of it and warms himself; he kindles a fire and bakes bread. Also he makes a god and worships it; he makes it an idol and falls down before it. Half of it he burns in the fire. Over the half he eats meat; he roasts it and is satisfied. Also he warms himself and says, "Aha, I am warm, I have seen the fire!" And the rest of it he makes into a god, his idol, and falls down to it and worships it. He prays to it and says, "Deliver me, for you are my god!"

It takes real insight to know which end of a log is for fuel and which is for worship. The poor guy probably minored in this kind of thing at Canaanite Community College only to have Isaiah make fun of him.

Understandably, for many people with the bracelets, this kind of thing does not sound like something Jesus would do. Or would he? Would Jesus tell a joke or—even more controversial—mock someone?

In the closing line of his classic book *Orthodoxy*, G. K. Chesterton claims that "there was some one thing that was too great for God to show us when He walked upon the earth; and I have sometimes fancied that it was His mirth."[20] According to Chesterton, the one thing Jesus was not was funny. On this point, though, Chesterton is wrong.

Conversely, Elton Trueblood says, "There are numerous passages . . . which are practically incomprehensible when regarded as sober prose, but which are luminous once we become liberated from the gratuitous assumption that Christ never joked. . . . Once we realize that Christ was not always engaged in pious talk, we have made an enormous step on the road to understanding."[21] Trueblood goes on to say, "Christ laughed, and . . . He expected others to laugh. . . . A misguided piety has made us fear that acceptance of His obvious wit and humor would somehow be mildly blasphemous or sacrilegious. Religion, we think, is serious business, and serious business is incompatible with banter."[22]

Jesus was funny. A few funny snippets from God's Word will suffice to show the humor of Jesus. Jesus once said it was easier for a camel to pass through the eye of a needle than for a rich man to enter heaven (Matt. 19:24). Rather than seeing the humor, some guys educated beyond their intelligence with no sense of humor try to explain that there was a small doorway in a wall somewhere called the needle that camels would have to shimmy under to pass through. But what Jesus meant was that it's hard for rich guys to go to heaven, and he said it in a funny way that some Bible commentators don't understand, which makes it even funnier.

Jesus was funny when he mocked the guy with a two-by-four sticking out of his head who, rather than running to the emergency room, spent his time criticizing people who had a speck of sawdust in their eye (Matt. 7:3). Jesus actually mocked the fact that some people prayed in public to get a crowd as if they were some kind of prayer rock star (Matt. 6:5). He mocked the fact that some people liked to suck their faces in when they were fasting so that people would ask them if they were supermodels or just holy (Matt. 6:16). He also mocked the guys who tithed out of their spice racks but forgot not to be jerks (Matt. 23:23).

Jesus' humor helps us understand the words of Matthew 15:12: "Then the disciples came and said to him, 'Do you know that the Pharisees were offended when they heard this saying?'" Really? The guys to whom Jesus said their moms shagged the devil were offended? In Matthew 11:6 Jesus says, "Blessed is the one who is not offended by me." The only way to not be offended by Jesus is to realize that we are all silly sinners who need to repent, laugh at ourselves, and take God seriously but not ourselves.

The objection is often raised that Jesus did mock people but we should not because we are not Jesus and are not perfect like him or perfectly inspired by the Holy Spirit like the Old Testament prophets were. In response to this objection, Douglas Wilson says,

> . . . and so consequently we had better be safe than sorry. But *safe* by what standard? *Sorry* by what standard?
>
> The problem here is that "the rule" applies equally to everything that Jesus did and all that the apostles and prophets wrote. . . . We will be imperfect as we imitate love, grace, forgiveness, kindness, rebuke, sarcasm, gentleness, and so on. Therefore we ought not to strive to be godly at all. We must remain in our ungodliness for fear that an attempt to be godly may result in ungodly failure. . . .
>
> The retort may then come back that we simply apply "the rule" to hard-hitting comments, satire, sarcasm, and so forth. But this begs the question: What standard are we using to say we should imitate *this* part of Christ's demeanor and refuse to imitate *that* part of it? What standard do we use to assemble this hierarchy of verbal values? Why do we say, "Imitate Christ in His kindness to the tax gatherers, but *never* imitate Him in His treatment of the religiously pompous?" Why not the reverse? "*Always* make fun of religious wowsers, but never imitate Christ's kindness to the downtrodden." This kind of selectivity is not approaching the Scriptures as the Word of God but rather belongs to the "scissors and library paste" school of hermeneutics.[23]

Perhaps even more controversial than humor is the biblical usage of strong language. The Bible does, on rare occasions, use very strong language to portray self-righteousness and the religions that promote it in the most disgusting of terms. The Bible does this because religion that promotes self-righteousness by one's own works is anathema to the gospel; the only righteousness we have is not merited to us by works but gifted to us by grace through Jesus Christ. Therefore, the Bible uses graphic and disturbing imagery to show how vile to God are religion and self-righteous works done in a vain effort to make oneself acceptable in the sight of a perfectly holy and righteous God.

One example from the Old Testament is Isaiah 64:6, which says, "We have all become like one who is unclean, and all our righteous deeds are like a polluted garment." The *Pulpit Bible Commentary* says that the literal meaning of the language in this verse is "as a menstruous garment."[24]

Our study takes us to the verse in the New Testament that should have a wick attached to it for all the debate that has blown up around it. Speaking of his religiously self-righteous way of life before meeting Jesus, Paul says, "Indeed, I count everything as loss because of the surpassing worth of knowing Christ Jesus my Lord. For his sake I have suffered the loss of all things and count them as rubbish, in order that I may gain Christ" (Phil. 3:8). That little word "rubbish" has been the source of big controversy. Various English translations use words such as "rubbish," "garbage," "filth," "dung," "refuse," "worthless trash," and "dog dung." Making the entire issue more difficult is that the word is a *hapax legomenon*, which means it appears only once in the entire New Testament.

Greek scholar and expert Daniel B. Wallace[25] has studied this word in great detail, and he explains: "In Phil 3:8, the best translation of *skuvbala* seems clearly to be from the first group of definitions [that is, meaning (human) excrement]. The term conveys both revulsion and worthlessness in this context. In hellenistic Greek it seems to stand somewhere between 'crap' and 's**t.'"[26]

What Isaiah and Paul are pointedly declaring is that the good works of everyone from devout Oprah followers to the Jehovah's Witness grandmas who knock on doors so that they will be good enough for God to love them—along with the family who thinks they are better than everyone else and able to stand before God on the day of judgment because they avoided alcohol and tobacco and had a lot of kids they homeschooled well and shielded from all television by keeping the girls busy knitting denim jumpers and the boys active learning the trivium—are as cherished a gift to God as a bloody tampon or a pile the dog leaves in the yard. Why? Because any effort to justify oneself in the sight of God rather than depending solely upon the person and work of Jesus as the grounds for our righteousness is a bloody mess and a steaming pile.

At this point, we can either argue with the Scriptures or consider their relevance for our own life. My sincere hope is that we all learn to deal with the speck in our eye before we start using our words, including the ones we blog and text-message, to criticize the words of others. For that to happen, we must see that shepherds and sheep alike are prone to moments and seasons of acting like swine, wolves, and dogs. When the Old Testament prophets attack the idolaters, they are speaking about us. When Jesus lampoons the Pharisees, his words are for us. And when Paul skewers the Judaizers, he is thinking of us.

We love it when "those guys" get verbally shot. But we hate it when "our guys" get verbally shot. Why? Because we wrongly think that "those guys" are always the bad guys and "our guys" are always the good guys. However, at varying times and in varying ways to varying degrees we are all religious dogs, and the first step toward safeguarding ourselves is to accept this fact humbly and not only repent of our sin but also of our religious righteousness.

Pray for the Shepherds

Sheep need to be fed, swine need to be rebuked, wolves need to be shot, and dogs need to be beaten. Most of this work is to be done by the shepherds. So the shepherds need prayer.

If you are a shepherd, you know that you need prayer. If you are a sheep, please do pray for your shepherd so that your heart would be tender toward him, and his heart would be tender toward God and God's sheep. It would be most helpful to your shepherd if, before you rush to criticize him, you would spend time in prayer for him. In fact, you should pray for your shepherd more than you criticize him.

As you consider how to pray for him rather than criticize him, it will be most helpful if you would think about his context. Just as the Old Testament prophets were at war with the Canaanites, Jesus had the Pharisees in the clinch, Paul was looking for the Judaizers' jaws, John was grappling with Gnosticism, and Luther was pounding the pope, your shepherd may be in quite a battle for his flock. A prayer partner is sometimes all it takes to keep love in his heart, home in his head, and steel in his spine.

Throughout the New Testament Paul often asks people to pray for him (Col. 4:3; 1 Thess. 5:25; 2 Thess. 3:1). He is often painfully honest about his poverty, illness, struggles, frustrations, betrayals, imprisonments, and needs. In fact, many of us shepherds who consider ourselves Pauline in our doctrine are sadly, woefully deficient in being Pauline in our humble request for pointed prayer. Nonetheless, faithful friends of the gospel are often a great assistance when they simply pray because the Holy Spirit has prompted them, and when they also kindly and sincerely seek out particular ways to pray for their shepherds. For you who are faithful to pray for your shepherd or who in reading this aspire to join the faithful, I encourage you to pray for your shepherd in seven ways.

1) *Please pray that God would give your shepherd a discerning mind.* Your shepherd needs to discern who the sheep, swine, wolves, and dogs are so that he knows how he and the church should respond. Subsequently, he needs the wisdom of Solomon to shepherd his flock well. Thankfully James 1:5 says that if we ask God for discerning wisdom, God will hear and answer our prayer; so please pray accordingly for your shepherd.

2) *Please pray that God would give your shepherd thick skin.* Critics can be merciless, and Judas-like friends can be even crueler. Your shepherd receives mean-spirited e-mails from the people he cares for, suffers from constant gossip and rumors about him and his family, and spends hours every day simply turning the other check. When he fails, he is criticized for being a poor leader. And when he succeeds, he is criticized by those who are jealous. When he is young, he is criticized for being inexperienced and arrogant. And when he is old, he is criticized for not being as energetic, passionate, and innovative as when he was young.

Every shepherd invariably winds up with his face in his tear-stained hands, and the sheep who never see this are well served to know it. Some of us shepherds have incredibly thick skin and still suffer with seasons of depression. Shepherds with thin skin suffer constantly and terribly. Often only their wives and fellow shepherds know of their pain; they are reticent to share it with the sheep in their flock because wolves and dogs are also in the flock, and such weakness only rouses their thirst for blood as they devise ways to attack the shepherd so they can devour the flock. So please pray that your shepherd would have thick skin and selective hearing to ignore the people and comments he should—and yet to receive the people and comments he should.

3) *Please pray that your shepherd would have a good sense of humor.* Without a good sense of humor, shepherds will be overcome with anxiety and stress and will miss wonderful opportunities to laugh deeply from the gut as an act of faith. Shepherds are imperfect as are their individual sheep and collective flock. Ministry is pressure, and humor is a good and holy release valve that helps to relieve the pressure. Without the release valve of humor, the pressure on a shepherd increases until he simply breaks. This break will be spiritual, emotional, mental, or physical, depending upon where the weakest cracks are in his life. Too many shepherds break. Some leave ministry altogether, while others limp along as their outlook grows bleaker, darker, and more somber.

4) *Please pray that your shepherd would have a tender heart.* Over time, a shepherd is prone to become calloused. This callousness is often simply a survival tactic employed by a shepherd who is otherwise uncertain that he can persevere in his calling. One of the primary duties of shepherds is to see and deal with sin, folly, and horror in the lives of people they love. It is brutal. If you are not a shepherd, imagine spending much of every week visiting the sick and dying in the hospital, preaching funerals, mending broken marriages, serving addicts of various ills, and weeping with victims of molestation and rape. The needs are overwhelming, the shepherd feels woefully unfit for the work, and there is no end in sight. In order to survive, a shepherd can callous his heart, withdraw from his people, or even battle fits of angry rage. So please pray that his heart would remain tender toward God and his flock, because that requires a miracle of grace.

5) *Please pray that your shepherd would have a humble disposition.* Shepherds are notoriously proud and, by the grace of God, need to continually pursue humility. More than once the New Testament states that God opposes the proud and gives grace to the humble (James 4:6; 1 Pet. 5:5), and twice Proverbs declares that God actually hates pride (Prov. 6:16–17; 8:13). Proverbs goes on to declare that if humility is not learned, then God imposes humiliation as chastening discipline (Prov. 16:5, 18). Simply put, pride is the root that nourishes the fruit of all sin and is akin to picking a fight with God. But God promises to give grace to the humble. Nothing breaks a church like pride, and nothing builds it like humility. Jesus the Chief Shepherd is the most perfectly humble person who has or will ever live.

Under Jesus, the shepherd of the flock (or pastor) is to set an example for the flock in humility. This means the humble shepherd will consider others' needs above his own and labor for the fame of Jesus above the goodness of his own name or ministry performance. Without this humility, a proud shepherd contributes to a church culture of rivalry, conceit, competition, and selfish ambition, and a lack of teachability, submission to godly authority, and repentance.

As you pray for the humility of your shepherd, pray that as a result of humility he would follow the truth wherever it leads, invite and pursue correction from fellow shepherds, have the courage to lead boldly despite the personal cost, learn from everyone, repent quickly and thoroughly, seek and celebrate God's grace at work in the lives of other Christians and churches, have a spirit of thankfulness, listen to Scripture more than himself, and sleep like a Calvinist, even if he is an Arminian.

6) *Please pray that your shepherd would have a supportive family.* Between the accusations of Satan, stings of critics, and discouraging awareness of his personal shortcomings and inadequacies, a shepherd is greatly served by an encouraging wife and a home in which the Holy Spirit's work is evident. Please also pray for the shepherd's wife, because she is often put under great demands to be friends with women in the church she does not enjoy, reveal details from her personal life with people she does not trust, attend parties with people she does not know, share her marriage and family with people she

does not feel appreciated by, endure gossip from people she has not met, and lovingly serve people who are not thankful.

Also pray for the shepherd's children. If they are struggling with sin and faith, there is great pressure on them to hide it so that their father retains the respect of the sheep and so that the swine do not have an opportunity to gloat and call their father a hypocrite, the wolves do not have an opportunity to attack their father, and the dogs do not have an opportunity to bark at their father. A pastor should aspire for his wife and children to be nothing more or less than mature Christians, so please pray that they, like everyone else in the flock, would be able to experience sanctification in a loving church.

7) *Please pray that your shepherd would have an evangelistic devotion.* People are dying and going to hell without Jesus. It is easy in light of the needs of the sheep, folly of the swine, dangers of the wolves, and threats of the dogs for the shepherd to become so consumed with his flock that he does not seek the conversion of lost people. So please pray for your shepherd that he would have a heart for lost people and make time in his schedule to labor for their salvation.

It seems fitting to let God's Word have the last word about our words:

> An evil man is ensnared by the transgression of his lips,
>   but the righteous escapes from trouble.
> From the fruit of his mouth a man is satisfied with good,
>   and the work of a man's hand comes back to him.
> The way of a fool is right in his own eyes,
>   but a wise man listens to advice.
> The vexation of a fool is known at once,
>   but the prudent ignores an insult.
> Whoever speaks the truth gives honest evidence,
>   but a false witness utters deceit.
> There is one whose rash words are like sword thrusts,
>   but the tongue of the wise brings healing.
> Truthful lips endure forever,
>   but a lying tongue is but for a moment. (Prov. 12:13–19)

CHAPTER FIVE

Story-shaped Faith

Daniel Taylor

"IN THE BEGINNING, God . . . " (Gen. 1:1).

"There was once a man in the land of Uz whose name was Job" (Job 1:1).

"Now in those days a decree went out from Caesar Augustus" (Luke 2:1).

"There came a man sent from God, whose name was John" (John 1:6).

"Jesus said, 'A man was going down from Jerusalem to Jericho, and fell among robbers'" (Luke 10:30).[1]

God is telling the world a story. It begins in eternity past and stretches into eternity future. It climaxed two thousand years ago when God entered into his creation in a new way. It could reach its temporal conclusion today—or in five thousand years. The theme of the story is *shalom*: all things in their created place doing what they were created to do in loving relationship with their creator. And, amazing grace, it is a story into which God invites you and me as characters.

Human beings are story-shaped creatures. We are born into stories, raised in stories, and live and die in stories. Whenever we have to answer a big question—who am I, why am I here, what should I do, what happens to me when I die?—we tell a story. The Ur-story, the foundational story, is the story of God's love for his creation, and all other stories are to be measured against it. The single best way of conceiving of faith, and of a faithful life, is as a story in which you are a character. Your life task is to be a character in the greatest story every told. It is what you were created for.

If faith were primarily an idea, the intellect alone might be adequate for dealing with it. Since it is instead a life to be lived, we need story. Story, as does life, engages all of what we are—mind, emotions, spirit, body. Faith calls us to live in a certain way, not just to think in a certain way. It is no surprise, then, that the central record of faith in human history opens with an unmistakable story signature: "In the beginning . . . "

A Story from My Life

I will begin a defense of all these claims with a story from my own life. My earliest memories of movies were formed in drive-in theaters. It was at a drive-in, in the 1950s, in Santa Barbara, California, out by the airport, that I first witnessed the parting of the Red Sea.

Don't think you understand the parting of the Red Sea until you've seen it through the eyes of a nine-year-old on a huge outdoor screen through your car windshield, holding a bucket of butter-wet popcorn. Charleton Heston stood up on that rock, with the weaselly Edward G. Robinson whining about the approaching Egyptian army, and he said something about the power of the Lord and raised his staff and—yousers!—the waters boiled for a moment and then separated into towering walls on either side of a strip of dry land. Then the nation of Israel marched right through the middle of the sea!

It was enough to make me stop chewing on the popcorn and start chewing on the idea that God was God and that, when he wanted to, he could do eye-popping things.

Compare that experience with presenting a nine-year-old boy with the following proposition: "God is powerful." Certainly true. Nothing I would disagree with, then or now. But also nothing that would make me stop chewing on my popcorn.

"God is powerful" is a proposition, an abstract declaration of fact. It elicits an intellectual assessment—true or false. It tells us something important, but in a very limited way. A story *showing*—better, embodying—that God is powerful, engages not just our intellect, but our whole person.

When I saw those waters part, I felt it in my stomach as well as in my brain. My breath caught and my pulse quickened just a bit. I was not just seeing something, much less just thinking something;

I was experiencing something. I was, for those moments, in the middle of a story—in fact, in the middle of the sea—standing with those frightened Jews, caught up in a miracle. And it was literally awesome. It is now many years and a few educational degrees later. I can reason as carefully as the next fellow. I understand the value of propositions and evidence. I still believe we must start with the stories.

Stories Are from God

Stories are God's idea. God is the one who created story—the form of story—and us as story-shaped creatures. He has chosen story as the primary way to present himself to his creation. The Bible does not simply contain stories; it reflects God's choice of the form of story as the primary means by which to tell us about himself and how to be in right relationship with him. It is also the form God has chosen to preserve that knowledge over many, many generations.

Consider, for instance, the story in the book of Joshua of a second miraculous crossing of water in the Old Testament. It is not as famous as the crossing of the sea in Egypt forty years earlier, but just as instructive. This is the crossing of the Jordan River into the Promised Land. Moses has died and the nation of Israel is now under the leadership of Joshua (a leader, by the way, being primarily a steward of a story). They arrive at the river and find it at flood stage. How are they going to get across?

God tells Joshua to have the priests carrying the ark of the covenant step into the river. When they do so the river stops flowing, and they stand in the middle of the riverbed while the entire nation crosses. When everyone has crossed, God does an interesting thing. He tells Joshua to appoint one person from each tribe and have them go back into the riverbed where the priests are standing and for each of them to pick up a stone.

They are to make a monument of these stones on the other side "to serve as a sign among you. In the future, when your children ask you, 'What do these stones mean?' tell them that the flow of the Jordan was cut off before the ark of the covenant of the LORD. . . . These stones are to be a memorial to the people of Israel forever" (Josh. 4:6–7).

This is a passage about the importance of memory, about the

importance of telling stories. The nation of Israel had a problem with memory lapses. The prophets (who were primarily storytellers) were always telling them to remember the stories of the past because they were the key to the present and future. Think of the prophet Joel commanding the people: "Tell it to your children, and let your children tell it to their children, and their children to the next generation" (Joel 1:3).

When Israel remembered the stories that told them who they were, where they had come from, and who their God was, they prospered. When they quit telling the stories, they no longer understood who they were, and they invited disaster. And the same is true with us.

This is why Joshua ordered each of the tribes of Israel to contribute a rock to commemorate God's provision for them in leading them across the river Jordan. The rock monument in their midst is a story prompt. It will cause the children of the next generation to ask, "Why are these rocks here?" That question will prompt the story, and a new generation will understand the power of God.

Stories and Propositions

This story in Joshua ends with these words: "He did this so that all the nations of the earth may know that the hand of the LORD is powerful and so that you may always fear the LORD your God" (4:24).

The Lord is powerful. That is a proposition. A declaration of fact. A statement.

It is true. But by itself it doesn't have a lot of impact. It hangs suspended in the land of abstract assertion. To be meaningful to human beings, it must be given the body and blood of story.

How do we *know* the Lord is powerful? Let me tell you a story.

What does it *mean* to say "the Lord is powerful"? Let me tell you a story.

Let me tell you a story about the time the nation of Israel crossed the Jordan River into the Promised Land . . . , a story about the time Gideon routed the enemies of Israel with a handful of men . . . , a story about the feeding of five thousand people . . . , *the* story about the empty tomb.

Propositions are important. The Lord *is* powerful. The Lord *is* good. Jesus *is* the Son of God. Christ *did* rise from the dead. But propositions depend on the stories out of which they arise for their power and meaning and practical application. The story provides the existential foundation on which the proposition rests. If no story, then no significance for the proposition.

Imagine having all the propositions of the Bible but none of the stories. No Genesis or Exodus, none of the historical books of the Old Testament, no Gospels, no Acts—only Romans, parts of the Epistles, and scattered assertions and commands from here and there. Those assertions and commands would still be true, but we would have very little idea of what to do with them.

Belief is a whole-body, whole-life experience. No one believes anything important with the intellect alone. If only the intellect is involved, it is not belief but merely an idea. That is another reason why we do well to think of faith as a story in which we are characters. Faith, like stories, engages us as whole persons, not as parts.

Belief or faith enlists all the various aspects of the mind—intellect, analysis, intuition, memory, curiosity, imagination. It also engages the emotions—desires, affections, fears. And believing also involves the will—intention, purpose, resolve, motivation, perseverance. Further, what and how we believe is influenced by personality, temperament, and character. And, yes, by the body, as shown by my boyhood reaction to Charlton Heston parting the waters.

And, of course, all the things above are deeply influenced by our life experiences. Our beliefs about God, right and wrong, life and death—and about endless specific issues such as abortion, terrorism, race, immigration, homosexuality, the role of women, and so on—cannot be separated from thousands of life experiences, conscious and unconscious, subtle and overt. And we capture these experiences in story.

How obtuse then to think that we arrive, or even should arrive, at our important beliefs through any single faculty, least of all through leaky reason. Reason is a powerful tool, but it is a tool that will serve any master, including the most odious. We do well to reason as clearly as we can, but we are foolish to pretend that reason alone or any other single mental function can tell us what is true, what is important, what to believe, or how to live.

Do not organize your life around anything that values only one aspect of what you are. If it respects only the reason, it is inadequate. If it appeals only to the emotions, it will let you down. If it values only will power and discipline, it will crack and crumble. Instead, you and I need a story to live by that takes seriously every aspect of what we are as created beings.

Propositions are shorthand for the stories. When we are trying to explain something or correct something, we often cannot take the time to tell all the relevant stories. So instead we use the proposition—the short, hopefully clear assertion. The proposition stands in for the stories, but the propositions also depend on the stories for their ultimate significance.

Fortunately, neither God nor the Bible asks us to choose between propositions and stories. We are provided both, because both have their purpose. Stories and propositions need each other. Each provides a limit that the other must respect—a kind of mutual check.

The propositional truth acts as a check on how we interpret a story. Consider, for instance, the story of Christ's crucifixion. A fashionable interpretation of that story in some academic circles sees it as a story of divine child abuse, an angry parent demanding the sacrifice of his child to appease his wrath. In this case, it is helpful to test that interpretation against the assertion, clearly stated throughout the Bible, that God is love. The proposition that God is love, distilled from many stories, should cause us to reject as false this absurd interpretation of this particular master story.

Similarly, a story (or stories) acts as a check in how we interpret and apply certain propositions. The Bible teaches clearly that God hates sin and punishes sinners. That truth, however, needs to be understood and lived out in light of stories such as that of the woman caught in adultery. In that story, Jesus rejects both the legalist, when he tells the woman "neither do I condemn you," and the relativist, when he says "go and sin no more." Stories offer the richness and specificity and motivation necessary to keep the proposition from being merely abstract, reductionist, inert, shallow, or legalistic.

Furthermore, it is helpful to see that the propositions of the Bible are usually *embedded* in a story. The Ten Commandments, the most famous assertions of all, arise within the story of the people of Israel in the wilderness. Why these ten? There are hundreds of other commands in the Old Testament, so why highlight these ten at this time? One possibility is that they are the ones most needed at this point in Israel's collective story. Israel has come out of a nation with many gods and is surrounded by other nations with many more. They need to keep uppermost in their minds that there is only one God and that he is jealous of their worship. Likewise, they are living in intense community—on an extended road trip together, for better or worse. So they need commands about how to get along within the same tent (with father and mother) and with those in the next tent (with the temptations to envy, theft, adultery, and even murder).

The point is that there are very few propositions in the Bible, and in life generally, that do not originate in and depend upon stories. We are told in Deuteronomy 4, for instance, that "the LORD your God is a merciful God; he will not abandon you or destroy you or forget the covenant he swore with your ancestors" (v. 31). Note how the assertion about God's mercy, an abstract proposition, is tied both to their past ("ancestors") and future ("will not abandon") stories. Stories and propositions interact to create life-shaping meaning.

Some who emphasize the centrality of narrative in the Bible do so because they are nervous about truth claims. If we can just call them stories, they reason, we can set aside troublesome questions about historical truth (did these stories take place in time and space?) and focus on other kinds of truth—psychological, symbolic, or spiritual. I see the attraction, but I'm not interested. If Christ did not physically rise from the grave, then he joins a huge crowd of "good people" who at most provide us with distant "examples." If he did rise, he is the Savior of the world. That's a reality-changing difference, and I am not interested in using the concept of story to blur it.

Others, however, want to define faith primarily in terms of assent to propositions. Give us a list of assertions about God and if we agree to them we are believers—people of faith. These people get nervous when you talk about story, because they suspect, not without reason, that you want to turn faith into a weak broth of comforting tales and do-goodism. Their antidote is vigorous assent to clear assertions about God and his creation.

One problem with this approach is that, by itself, it does no more than put you in company with the demons. In the book of James, we

are told a bit sarcastically, "You believe that God is one. You do well;
the demons also believe, and shudder" (2:19). Mere assent to a set of
propositions is not a demonstration of faith.

There is more than one way to fall off this horse. Separate stories
from historicity and a high standard of truth and you turn the most
important stories into mere illustrations. On the other hand, separate
propositions from stories and you turn them into abstract ideas,
uprooting them from the soil that gives them life. Instead, we should
affirm the core propositions but never let them get far from the stories
and from our own participation as characters in that story.

Passing on the Stories

The Bible understands that stories are not only central to faith, but
they are also the natural carriers of faith from one generation to the
next. The people in the Old Testament are constantly reminded of
their master story—they are the people God rescued out of Egypt—
and are admonished to shape their lives around that fact. Build
rock monuments by the Jordan as a story prompt, read the newly
rediscovered Scriptures by the wall of Jerusalem as you rebuild, hear
from the prophets the stories of God's faithfulness in the past and the
possibilities for the future. When God rescues you, tell the story, as
Psalm 102:18 instructs:

> Let this be recorded for a future generation,
>   that a people not yet created may praise the LORD.

Who is this future generation for which the story has been
recorded? It includes, among others, you and me. How is it we have
the opportunity to know the God who created us? Because someone
lived the story, and someone else told the story, and someone wrote
down the story, and others chose to repeat the story, and many were
willing to die for the story. And so, generation after generation after
generation, the story of God's love for his creation has been told—and
we are the beneficiaries.

Which prompts a question: *are we going to be the generation that
does not pass on the story?* Stories are never more than a generation
from extinction. Our institutions for the elderly are filled with stories

that are disappearing every day, just as the elderly are. So will the story of faith, unless we tell it—in ways that draw people to make that story their own.

The Bible is many things, but among the most important it is a big storybook devoted to memory. Not *memories* in the sentimental sense, but memory in the crucial sense of understanding where you come from and what you are to do. And the key to memory is story. The Bible is a book of stories in many different forms—poetry, biography, song, history, letters, and more. It is a collection of stories that are chapters of the one great story: the story of God and his love for his creation. This is the meaning, says the Bible, of the story we call human history: God made us, God loves us, God calls us. That is the master plot of the greatest story ever told.

If you do not understand this story, you will never correctly understand who you are or why you are here. Americans have a great preoccupation with the self—self-analysis, self-help, self-fulfillment, and on and on. Do you want to understand yourself? Do you want to know the meaning of life or what you are to do? Let me tell you a story: "In the beginning God . . . " That is the opening line of the story of God's relationship with his creation. It is the story by which all other stories, including our individual stories, are to be understood.

The Bible offers a master story that we are invited to make our personal story. We become characters in that story. If we join that story, we have both rights and responsibilities. One of those responsibilities is to remember what God has done and to tell it to the next generation.

The Power of Stories to Change Us

If you want evidence that stories involve us as whole persons—or that the use of story is central in the Bible—consider the story of David, Bathsheba, and the prophet Nathan as told in chapters 11 and 12 of 2 Samuel. This is an example from within the Bible itself of how stories shape us.

We start in the middle of an ongoing story. David has abused his power as king in order to sleep with Bathsheba and has made her pregnant. To cover his failure—morally and as a leader—he has her husband called back from war, assuming Uriah will sleep with his wife and thereby cover David's tracks. David, however, has not counted on Uriah's integrity and loyalty. When Uriah refuses the comforts of home while his fellow soldiers have none, David resorts to arranging for his death and brings Bathsheba into his household.

This is a powerful story in itself, and yet another story appears within the story that will signal a change in the direction of David's life and in that of the nation of Israel. God sends Nathan the prophet to David to tell him a story. The story is a trap or, perhaps better, an instrument for revelation.

And Nathan tells it masterfully, with a storyteller's sense of timing and irony and pathos. It goes like this:

> There were two men in a certain town—one rich and one poor. The rich man had great flocks and herds. The poor man had nothing but one little lamb he had bought. He raised that little lamb, and it grew up with him and his children. It ate from the man's meager fare and drank from his cup, and slept in his arms like a baby daughter. One day a traveler arrived at the home of the rich man, but he was unwilling to take an animal from his own flock or herd to prepare for the traveler. Instead, he took the poor man's lamb and prepared it for his guest. (2 Sam. 12:1–4)

Nathan's story has the "once upon a time" feel of fiction—"There were two men in a certain town"—more than of a recounting of an actual historical event, and yet David is totally engaged by the story. Historicity is crucial in some stories, but not in this one. Not all stories have to have happened to be true.

David is enraged by the actions of the rich man in Nathan's story and proclaims in all his royal indignation, "As surely as the LORD lives, the man who did this deserves to die!" *All* of David is engaged in this story: his intellect, his moral sense, his emotions, and, yes, his body (his heart no doubt is beating faster). That is, he responds to Nathan's story as a whole person—and it is exactly the response Nathan must have hoped for.

At this climactic moment, Nathan unleashes the lightning bolt of revelation as only a great story can. We can picture him reaching out his arm and pointing at David as he shouts, emphasizing each word—"*You* . . . are . . . that . . . man!"

Nathan then makes explicit the connection between the story he's told and David's story:

David is the rich man and Uriah the poor.
David has been given much and yet has taken from the man
who has little.
David has been blessed by God, and he has responded by
breaking God's law.

This story about David and Nathan shows not only that God uses stories and that we are wired to make and respond to stories, but it also shows that stories are about choices and their consequences—as is the life of faith.

The essence of stories is characters making choices, especially characters making difficult choices with uncertain outcomes. "What will happen if he opens that door?" "Which suitor will she choose?" "How will Solomon decide which woman the baby belongs to?" It is the tension of choices that draws us to story. And there is always the implicit question: "What would I do if I were in this situation—if it were my story?"

In the Bathsheba story, David makes disastrous choices and they have disastrous consequences: a woman abused, a faithful subject murdered, a baby dead, the character of the king compromised and therefore the community put at risk (Nathan tells him that because of his sin, Israel will never know peace in his lifetime)—all because David isn't satisfied with everything God has given him. He wants more; he wants something else. But this story also indicates yet another quality of story: stories have the power to change us. And what is faith about if it isn't about changed lives? David's failure and its consequences are revealed by a story, but it should also be pointed out that Nathan's story also leads David to repent.

David is shown his own story within Nathan's story, and, unlike his predecessor Saul, he reacts appropriately. He says, "I have sinned against the LORD." That confession spares his life. And although it does not save him and Bathsheba from the loss of their son, it makes possible the subsequent birth of Solomon, the son who will eventually carry on his line.

Powerful stories have this potential to change us. They do not exist to kill time but to redeem the time. They are quite aggressive in a sense. They say, "You must be different because of what you have heard. Your life cannot be the same now that you know this story." David could not hear Nathan's story—and Nathan's interpretation of the story—and pretend he could go about his normal business. He might be king, but kings must pay heed to stories too.

And the same is true of the gospel story. Once we have heard it, we are not allowed to stay the same. The gospel story judges our story and finds it wanting. It is a judgment we are invited to accept or reject. If we accept it, then we choose, like characters in a story, to change the plot of our lives. In so doing we do not give up who we are; we become more of who we are, that is, more of who we were always meant to be.

The most important stories are, in this sense, directive. They tell us we must be different and we must change, and they often tell us how we must change. The contemporary philosopher Alasdair MacIntyre argues that stories from many sources tell children what life is like and what role they are to play in it. "Deprive children of stories," he claims, "and you leave them unscripted, anxious stutterers in their actions as in their words."[2] Stories teach us our lines.

Story logic dictates that if we know our lines, then we are responsible for saying them. That is, we must act. Nothing kills a story faster than a passive protagonist. Characters must act for a story to have meaning, even if they act disastrously. This is another reason why it is helpful to see faith as a story to be lived rather than just a set of propositions to be believed.

Some suggest it is illegitimate to act in faith if one has doubts, if one is uncertain. "I am not sure about what I believe, so it would lack integrity, even be hypocritical, for me to say I am a Christian and try to act accordingly." Story says otherwise. Characters in stories continually act with less than complete knowledge or certainty, including in stories of faith. Abraham set out on his life journey "not knowing where he was going" (Heb. 11:8). Moses was sure he was unqualified for the job God assigned him. "Send Aaron," he begged. Even Jesus pleaded in the garden of Gethsemane for a change, if possible, in the plot of his story.

If faith is primarily an intellectual puzzle to be solved, based on verifying a set of propositions, then perhaps we are justified in waiting to act until we have solved the puzzle. Every serious question about what we believe—and those questions are endless—offers an excuse to wait and think some more before acting.

Story, on the other hand, tells us that we have things to do—doubts or no doubts. This train is about to move out of the station. Get on board. Bring your doubts with you. There's room. But you must get on board—or not. You must, to change to the most common biblical metaphor, walk this path. The form of story is rich and deep and flexible enough to contain mystery and ambiguity and paradox and uncertainty and, yes, even your doubts. It's why, as human beings and as people of faith, we keep returning to stories.

Rachael's Story

I began these reflections with a story, and I will end with one. This is a story about a young woman named Rachael. I got to know her when she joined a group of students that I took to Cuba to study writing and Hemingway and to get away from a Minnesota January.

I have in front of me three photographs from Rachael's wedding day, taken not too long after that trip to Cuba. The first photograph is of a serious Rachael on her solemn day—solemn in the medieval sense of the word, meaning (as Thomas Howard reminds us) both joyous and weighted with significance, as in a solemn occasion, like a wedding or a coronation. In the second photograph Rachael is laughing extravagantly, as she often did. She is standing in her long wedding dress, looking down at her new husband, taking pleasure in him and in the occasion.

I believe that Rachael could laugh this way not only because it was part of her personality, but because she had a story to live by. She was not just a believer, someone who believed certain assertions about life; she was someone deeply and passionately caught up in God's story for the world and her part in it. Rachael was incurably curious; she was smart, she wrote excellent poems, she did everything she could to squeeze all the juice out of life.

When she was a child, a teacher asked her to identify something she was afraid of. She wrote, "I am afraid of having a mediocre life." And she lived so as to defeat mediocrity: she went twice to Spain and

with us to Cuba; she was game for any adventure—physical or intellectual or spiritual. She was devoted to friendship and to literature,
and she soaked herself in Bible study and prayer with a kind of discipline rare among Christians of any age. Rachael actually thought
it was possible to be godly—that is, to live her life in the reality of
God—and she thought she should try.

When she went to Spain the second time, she told her best friend
that they could not e-mail each other but only write letters, because
letters meant more. Her biggest fear in life was missing out on anything that life had to offer, especially missing something because she
was afraid to fail or was passive or indifferent. She had all the energy
and intensity and idealism of youth and yet, somehow, it didn't seem
naïve. Those who knew her got the feeling she had some wisdom
about ultimate things that we did not, and that it was our skepticism
that was naïve.

From Spain she wrote the following to her friend:

> Remember: as far as I understand it in this world, it's not good
> versus evil, love versus hate. No! It's love versus nothing. So fight
> against nothing, the mass *nada*. Love against the lack of love.
>
> Hope. Hope because there just might be a tomorrow. Hope
> brings into existence . . . that which we want to be. Don't accept
> the pessimism. Recognize the problem. Hope in God—"for I shall
> yet praise him."

And Rachael knew about being a character in God's story and
about having her own actions shaped by Christ's actions. When we
went to Cuba, I told the students to bring small gifts, practical things
like aspirin or writing pens or even bars of soap. When we were in
Santiago, Rachael was approached by a little boy, around four or five,
who asked her in Spanish for money—to buy some candy, he said.

Because she had committed herself to learning Spanish (German
and Japanese were next), she was ready for the question. She got
down on her knees so that she could look the little *niño* in the eye
and said to him in his own language, "I don't have any money, but
how would you like this?" And she pulled from her bag a shiny, new
baseball.

Living in a country where we saw poor kids playing baseball with a tree limb for a bat and wadded-up tape for a ball, his eyes got huge. He was so stunned by his good fortune that he could not move. It was a simple act of kindness, one quality of a healthy life story.

I have felt Rachael's kindness myself. Before we went to Cuba, she was in one of my classes. If you remember anything about school, you perhaps know that teachers sometimes get the feeling that no one is listening, no one is serious about learning, and they think that maybe, just maybe, they should have taken that job in advertising after all. Sometimes it shows on their faces or in little cynical comments they make in self-defense. Perhaps Rachael saw or heard that from me, as her teacher, one day. Whatever the reason, I found a handwritten poem on my door with no name on it. It ended something like this:

> Speak on, oh grey beard,
> Some of us are listening.

Rachael sent me this poem anonymously, as an encouragement. It was an act of kindness.

How do I know it was from her? I found out at a memorial reading we had for Rachael at our university, from her best friend, Amber, who helped her write it. For you see, the photographs from Rachael's wedding served double duty. They were also used on her funeral program a few months later.

Rachael had been to a shower for her soon-to-be sister-in-law, whom she told how thrilled she was to finally have a sister. And a few minutes after Rachael left the shower, her car was hit by a truck, and she was killed, sent suddenly into eternity. That third photograph from her wedding shows her leaving us—and so she did.

It is good that Rachael had a story to live by, because, unbeknownst to us (but not to her), it was chosen that her life be short. If Rachael had waited to find a story to live by, waited to have all her questions answered, she would never have found one at all.

Life is too precarious to live even a single day without a story.

In another of her letters from Spain, Rachael quotes from St. Teresa of Avila, "a saint to learn from in the short course of my life." She gives Teresa's words in Spanish and then translates them herself: "You must always remember that you don't have more than one soul, you have but to die one death, you have nothing more then one brief life, there is nothing more but one glory, and it is eternal, and so give your hands to many things."

Rachael gave her hands to many things, and so should we. She committed herself to a story, one that told her how to live, and she lived fully if not long, just as her Creator intended.

I attended Rachael's funeral with deep sadness and a great sense of loss. This was my second funeral for a former student at this same church, and as I sat at Rachael's funeral I also thought of Joe's, a young man who died of AIDS and who was full of faith and the acts of faith. Joe was sent off to heaven with a rock band and an audience that included people who did not look as if they often went to church. As we sent off Rachael to heaven, I thought of Joe, and I thought of the certainty that someday I will be the one in the casket at the front of the church.

How do I know Joe and Rachael went to heaven? How do I know there is such a place as heaven? How do I know there is a God who awaits you and me in heaven?

Because my story tells me so.

Other stories say it isn't so; it can't be so. You are free to choose those stories. I choose this one. I believe it is true—in all senses of the word—or I wouldn't choose it. I am glad this is my story. It lets me go to my students' funerals and sing and clap my hands.

CHAPTER SIX

Words of Wonder: What Happens When We Sing?

Bob Kauflin

SINGING. It's been a part of my life for as long as I can remember. I grew up on groups like the Swingle Singers, Association, and Beach Boys and sang in or accompanied choirs throughout high school and college. I was involved with the vocal group GLAD for thirty years and have been leading corporate worship for even longer. I can't imagine my life without singing.

Maybe you share my love for song. Then again, maybe you don't. You might be someone who patiently endures the singing on Sunday mornings until you hear what you really came for—the message.

If that's where you're at, Martin Luther wants to have a few words with you. Luther loved congregational music and considered music next to theology in importance.[1] He also had no problem saying what was on his mind. In a foreword to a collection of songs arranged for multiple voice parts, he wrote the following:

> When man's natural ability is whetted and polished to the extent that it becomes an art, then do we note with great surprise the great and perfect wisdom of God in music, which is, after all, His product and His gift; we marvel when we hear music in which one voice sings a simple melody, while three, four, or five other voices play and trip lustily around the voice that sings its simple melody and adorn this simple melody wonderfully with artistic musical effects,

thus reminding us of a heavenly dance where all meet in a spirit of friendliness, caress, and embrace. . . . A person who gives this some thought and yet does not regard it [music] as a marvelous creation of God, must be a clodhopper indeed and does not deserve to be called a human being; he should be permitted to hear nothing but the braying of asses and the grunting of hogs.[2]

We may not want to imitate Luther's attitude, but we *do* want to imitate his passion for singing—because God himself is passionate about singing.

God's Passion for Singing

God's heart for setting words to melodies is evident from even a casual reading of the Psalms.

> Oh sing to the LORD a new song;
>   sing to the LORD, all the earth.
> Sing to the LORD, bless his name;
>   tell of his salvation from day to day. (Ps. 96:1–2)

> Sing praises to God, sing praises!
>   Sing praises to our King, sing praises! (Ps. 47:6)

In just four verses we're commanded to sing *seven* times.

All told, the Bible contains over four hundred references to singing and fifty direct commands to sing. The longest book of the Bible, the Psalms, is a book of songs. And in the New Testament we're commanded not once, but twice, to sing psalms, hymns, and spiritual songs to one another when we meet (Eph. 5:19; Col. 3:16).

Why does God so often tell us not simply to praise him but to *sing* his praises when we meet? Why not just pray and preach? Why sing? Why are God's people throughout history always singing? Why words *and* music and not just words alone? Why does God want us to sing? One reason is that God himself sings. In Zephaniah 3:17 God exalts over his people "with loud singing." On the eve of his crucifixion, Jesus sang hymns with his disciples (e.g., Matt. 26:30). Hebrews 2:12 applies Psalm 22:22 to Jesus when it says, "In the midst of the congregation I will sing your praise." And Ephesians 5 tells us that one effect of being "filled with the Spirit" is "addressing one another in psalms and hymns and spiritual songs, singing and making melody to the Lord with your heart" (vv. 18–19).

We worship a triune God who sings, and he wants us to be like him.

How Music Relates to Words

There's more to say about why God wants us to sing, but first I want to make a few general comments about how music relates to words. When it comes to combining music and words, Christians tend to fall into one of three categories.

Some Christians think that music *supersedes the Word*, both in its significance and effect. They think that words without music—and that's usually a certain *kind* of music—are dry, unaffecting, and unimportant. They say things like, "Music speaks to me better than words can," or, "I can't worship unless I hear the style of music I like." For these folks, the impact of words is not only helped by music; it's dependent on it.

Other Christians think that music *undermines the Word*. As far as they're concerned, any time you combine music with words in the church, you're asking for problems. They fear the power that music seems to have over people, so they want to restrict its use.

Augustine acknowledged that struggle in his own soul. In his *Confessions* he wrote:

> I am inclined—though I pronounce no irrevocable opinion on the subject—to approve of the use of singing in the church, so that by the delights of the ear the weaker minds may be stimulated to a devotional mood. Yet when it happens that I am more moved by the singing than by what is sung, I confess myself to have sinned wickedly, and then I would rather not have heard the singing.[3]

Augustine was conscious of how music can distract us from the Word and potentially even undermine the Word. Ulrich Zwingli, a Swiss pastor who lived in the sixteenth century, went even further. He was so concerned about music's power that for a time he banned music from his meetings.

But music and the Word aren't meant to be in conflict with each other. God himself wants them together. That's why he tells us in

Psalm 147:1, "Praise the LORD! For it is good to sing praises to our God; for it is pleasant, and a song of praise is fitting." God didn't intend that music supersede the Word or that music undermine the Word. He gave us music to *serve the Word*. When that relationship is understood and appreciated, music becomes a powerful gift from God that complements, supports, and deepens the impact of the words we sing.

I'm going to take the rest of this chapter to describe three ways singing serves the Word and what difference it should make in our lives and our churches. My prayer is that by the end you'll understand better why God tells us so many times to *sing* to the Lord.

Singing Can Help Us Remember Words

The first thing music helps us do is *remember* words. Ever notice how easy it is to recall hymns you sang growing up—or a TV jingle from the eighties, nursery rhymes, Christmas carols, or pop songs that you learned as a teenager? Do you ever find yourself singing along to a song you hadn't heard for twenty years?

We store hundreds, literally thousands, of songs in our memory vaults, ready to be accessed at a moment's notice. Music has a powerful mnemonic ability that scientists are just beginning to understand. They're discovering that our minds are hardwired to recognize, categorize, and remember patterns in music better than we remember patterns in words alone.

For years Oliver Sacks has studied the effects of music on the brain. In his fascinating book *Musicophilia* he writes:

> Every culture has songs and rhymes to help children learn the alphabet, numbers, and other lists. Even as adults, we are limited in our ability to memorize series or to hold them in mind unless we use mnemonic devices or patterns—and the most powerful of these devices are rhyme, meter, and song.[4]

You see the power of music in Alzheimer's patients who can't tell you the name of their spouse or children but can instantly sing songs they learned as a child. That's partly because musical elements like rhythm, meter, and rhyme govern and restrict the way we say words and the time it takes to say them. And the more unique, repetitive, or immediately impacting these musical elements are, the easier it is to remember the song.

In Deuteronomy 31, God himself used music to help his people remember his words. As Israel was about to enter the Promised Land, God instructed Moses to teach Israel a song so that "when many evils and troubles have come upon them, this song shall confront them as a witness (for it will live unforgotten in the mouths of their offspring)" (Deut. 31:21). Singing can help us remember words.

Use Effective Melodies

What does music's mnemonic ability imply for us as followers of Christ? First, in the church we should use melodies that are effective. By "effective" I mean melodies that people are *able* to remember and melodies that people *want* to remember.

"Come Thou Fount of Every Blessing" is a hymn that's universally loved. Part of the reason it (and other great hymns) endure is that it's a well-crafted lyric set to a memorable, singable, and pleasing tune. If those same words were sung to a melody that was boring, unsingable, or forgettable, the hymn itself would never have become so popular.

Some people assume that the only effective melodies were written three hundred years ago. Others think that the best melodies have been written in the last ten years. Both groups are right. Both groups are wrong.

Some hymns have truly great melodies; they're memorable, singable, and enjoyable. But sometimes a melody or a musical setting begins to sound stale to a younger set of ears. The result is that generations end up leaving behind not only the music but the words.

New hymn versions aren't always as good as the originals, but some are as good and even better. Great hymn lyrics have been introduced to new audiences through fresh musical settings. It's always good to remember that the time period in which a tune was written isn't the ultimate determiner for its effectiveness for corporate worship.

Sing Words That God Wants Us to Remember

Here's another implication of music's ability to help us remember words: we should sing words that God wants us to remember. It not only matters *that* we sing; it matters *what* we sing. And the words we sing have a far greater impact on us than most of us are aware.

New Testament scholar Gordon Fee once said, "Show me a church's songs and I'll show you their theology." And it's true. Or as Mark Noll puts it, "We are what we sing."[5] Words should be the first thing we consider when we think about what songs to sing when we gather as the body of Christ.

In Colossians 3:16 Paul tells us that we are to "let the word of Christ dwell in you richly, teaching and admonishing one another in all wisdom, singing psalms and hymns and spiritual songs with thankfulness in your hearts to God." It is the Word of Christ, the Word about Christ, the Word of the gospel—not musical experiences or emotional highs—that are to dwell in us richly as we sing. There's certainly a place for expressing our subjective responses to God in song, but the greater portion of our lyrical diet should be the objective truths we're responding to: God's Word, his character, and his works, especially his work of sending his Son to be our atoning sacrifice.

That means the lyrics to our songs should reflect the broad themes of Scripture and not simply the themes we're fond of. Few understood this better than John and Charles Wesley. Charles wrote over 6500 hymns, and together they produced fifty-six hymnals that covered every area of Christian doctrine and experience that they taught. They weren't attempting to write worship hits. They wanted to teach and admonish the church. They wanted to give people songs that were filled with the Word of Christ. They understood that songs will never replace preaching but can serve as a significant complement to it.

So the question we need to ask today is this: if the teaching in our church was limited to the songs that we sing, how well taught would we be? How well would we know God? We should make it our aim not only to preach the whole counsel of God but to sing it, as well.

Seek to Memorize Songs

If singing can help us remember words, there's one more implication. We should seek to memorize songs. You've heard of A.D.D., Attention Deficit Disorder. Well, many Christians suffer from S.D.D., Screen Dependency Disorder. We know the words of the songs we're singing, but our eyes are glued to the screen, as though we'd be lost if the screen went blank. But songs don't come from the screen. They come from our hearts.

Others suffer from H.D.D., Hymnal Dependency Disorder. We've sung the same hymns for decades, and yet we'd never think of lifting our heads from the page for a few moments to sing out the glories of the Savior. I've found it helpful, whether I'm singing from a screen or a hymnal, to look at a line briefly and then look away and sing it. It helps me realize that God gave us music to help us remember words.

Singing Can Help Us Engage Emotionally with Words

Along with helping us remember words, singing also connects the words we sing with our hearts. In every culture and age, music is a language of emotion. It expresses, arouses, and speaks to our feelings. Music is capable of moving us in subtle and profound ways—in anticipated and unexpected ways—with or without words. As David played skillfully on his harp, Saul's troubled spirit was calmed (1 Sam. 16:23). In Matthew 11:17 Jesus referred to music that made people want to dance or mourn. God commands us to sing with thankfulness in our hearts to God (Col. 3:16). Our hearts should be involved because music is meant to affect us.

But why does music affect us so deeply? There are a number of reasons. Sometimes we're simply responding to musical principles that have been culturally learned. Personal experience with a song can affect its influence on us. We might assign moral value to songs, connecting them with aspects of our culture that we consider good or evil. We conclude that a certain beat, volume, chord progression, instrument, or vocal style is evil in and of itself. But unless those aspects are spelled out in Scripture we should be cautious about assigning a moral value to them. Another factor in a song's effect on us can be how a song is performed or led. If a performer or leader is inexperienced, out of tune, or out of sync, the music may not move us, or move us in the wrong ways. On the other hand, skill can make a song sound better than it actually is.

Whatever the reasons, music can come alongside words and heighten their emotional impact in a way we may not have perceived with words alone. That has a number of advantages. First, singing can help us take more time to reflect on the meaning of words. It can stretch out words and phrases. It can allow us to repeat them or put space in between words. All these qualities can help us engage emotionally with the words we're singing. For instance, singing, rather than reciting, the words to "Amazing Grace" enables us to stretch out and think more carefully about what we're singing. Likewise, the chorus to "It Is Well" gives us plenty of time to consider and enjoy the peace that God alone can bring to our souls. The music helps us engage with the words, "It is well with my soul." The mood of the music matches what we're saying. It's a peaceful, calming setting, and the music swells to this appropriate climax of confident trust: it *is* well with my soul.

Second, music can amplify the emotion of the words we're singing, whether it's joyful celebration ("Better Than Life"), reverent awe ("Holy, Holy, Holy"), or sorrowful repentance ("O Sacred Head Now Wounded"). Music serves as an additional influence that guides and deepens our emotional responses to the words we're singing. In one setting we might be mourning the death of Christ caused by our sins, and in another we might be joyfully celebrating the fact that his death has purchased our forgiveness and reconciled us to God. The music helps us know how to respond.

When talking about the emotional effect of music, we need to differentiate between being emotionally moved and spiritually enlightened. Music can move our emotions, but it can't speak propositional truth. You might say that music has a voice, but we're not always clear what that voice is saying. An instrumental piece can make us feel peaceful. But it can never tell us by itself that the Lord is our Shepherd or that Jesus endured God's wrath in our place so that we might have eternal peace with God. Only words can do that.

We Need a Broader Emotional Range in the Songs We Sing
If music is meant to help us engage emotionally with words, then most churches need a broader emotional range in the songs they sing. We need songs of reverence, awe, repentance, and grief as well as songs of joy, celebration, freedom, and confidence. The holiness of God cannot be adequately expressed in a two-minute up-tempo pop song. The jubilant triumph of Christ's victory over sin can't be fully communicated in a slow a cappella hymn.

There are varied traditions of song throughout history as well as very different hymn-writers: Puritans, psalm singers, pietists, charismatics, modern worship songs. Why do we need to pit them against one another? As long as the lyrics are edifying and faithful to Scripture, why can't we draw from each tradition to enable a broader range of emotional responses in corporate worship?

Singing Should Be an Emotional Event

If music is meant to stir our emotions, then it follows that singing should be an emotional event. For some of us, that's no problem. For others, it's a real struggle. If that's you, then listen to Jonathan Edwards's thoughts from his treatise on *Religious Affections*:

> The duty of singing praises to God seems to be appointed wholly to excite and express religious affections. No other reason can be assigned, why we should express ourselves to God in verse, rather than in prose, and do it with music, but only that such is our nature and frame, that these things have a tendency to move our affections.[6]

In other words, music is meant to affect us.

It's important to understand that when Jonathan Edwards uses the word *affections*, he's not merely talking about emotions. Emotions are included in the affections but not restricted to them. The affections he's referring to are more than momentary musical highs produced by hearing a beat or harmonic progression we find interesting. Edwards is speaking of *religious* affections, meaning our entire being is engaged with God and his truth in a way that determines our words, thoughts, choices, and actions. They spring from the center of our being.

Having said that, God is still worthy of our highest, purest, strongest emotions. Singing helps express and ignite them. Passionless singing is an oxymoron. John Wesley said it this way in an introduction to a hymnal:

> Sing lustily and with good courage. Beware of singing as if you were half-dead, or half asleep; but lift up your voice with strength. Be no more afraid of your voice now, nor more ashamed of its being heard, than when you sung the songs of Satan.[7]

Some of us are afraid of getting too emotional when we sing. But the problem isn't emotions. It's emotional*ism*. Emotionalism pursues feelings as ends in themselves. It's wanting to feel something with no regard for how that feeling is produced or its ultimate purpose. Emotionalism can also assume that heightened feelings are the infallible sign that God is present. They're not. The emotions that singing is meant to evoke are responses to the truths we're singing about God—his glory, his greatness, and his goodness. Vibrant singing enables us to connect truth about God seamlessly, with passion, so that we can combine doctrine and devotion, edification and expression, mind and heart.

Of course, we won't always be moved in the same way or to the same degree when we sing. We can sing theologically profound truths while thinking about what we're going to have for lunch or which teams are playing that afternoon. There will even be times when outward singing is accompanied by a numbness in our souls. What should we do? Rather than simply gritting our teeth and accepting that condition as normal, it's better to ask God for faith and mercy to feel what is appropriate in light of who God is and what he's done for us in Christ.

The good news is that God wants to use music, and has even designed music, to break through our apathy and hardness of heart, and to help us engage emotionally with his Word.

Singing Can Help Us Use Words to Demonstrate and Express Our Unity

We've seen how music can help us remember and engage emotionally with words. A final way singing serves words is by demonstrating and expressing our unity.

People sing together in the strangest places. At sporting events, fans sing enthusiastically about their desire to crush the opponent. People sing at New Year's Eve parties, Christmastime, rock concerts, weddings, and even funerals. When eating out we often have to endure well-meaning but musically challenged servers in restaurants attempt to sing some form of "Happy Birthday" to an embarrassed individual. I always ask myself, "Why do we do this?" It's not as though anyone thinks this is enjoyable. Do they?

While these events aren't equally significant, something similar is happening. Our singing tends to bind us together. It's more effective than simply reciting or shouting words in unison. Singing enables us to spend extended periods of time communicating the same thoughts, the same passions, and the same intentions. That process can actually have a physical effect on our bodies. Scientists have found that singing corporately produces a chemical change in our bodies that contributes to a sense of bonding.

When it comes to the church, this characteristic of singing has significant implications, all of which require great wisdom and discernment. To be clear, Scripture doesn't talk only about congregational singing. God is honored when we sing alone, when a musically gifted individual leads out in a solo, when a choir sings, or when different segments of a church sing to one another, taking turns. The Bible isn't specific about exactly who sings when.

But the predominant emphasis of Scripture is believers confessing their common beliefs together. The book of Revelation doesn't give the impression that Jesus died for independent soloists, people who would sing on their own clouds or in different sections of the renewed earth by themselves. He died to redeem a universal choir.

That means every voice in the church matters. We're not called simply to listen to others sing—as we are prone to do increasingly in our iPod-Internet-downloading culture—or to sing by ourselves. We are called to sing with others, especially in the context of our local church.

The question isn't, *Do you have a voice?* The question is, *Do you have a song?* If you've turned from your sins and trusted in the finished work of Christ, if you're forgiven and reconciled to God, then you have a song. It's a song of the redeemed, of those who have been rescued from the righteous wrath of God through the cross of Jesus Christ and are now called his friends. Once we were not a people, but now we are the people of God, and our singing together, every voice contributing, is one way we express that truth.

Sing Songs That Unite Rather than Divide the Church

What does this mean for the church? To begin with, we should seek to sing songs that unite rather than divide the church. We should appreciate—and, oh, how I do—the diverse musical genres and styles

that God has given to different cultures, ethnic groups, and generations. But music in the church was never meant to be "something for
everybody." That's not what we should be advertising.

There should be a common musical style that speaks to most
of the individuals in our church while occasionally introducing
new songs and styles, so that we might appreciate the glory of God
expressed in music in new ways. But the most important unifying
musical center should be the sound of the people themselves.

God commands us in numerous Scriptures to worship him with
instruments (Pss. 33:2–3; 81:2; 150). But dwarfing those commands
in number are the times God tells us to worship him with song. It
seems that the primary purpose for instruments is to support faith-
filled, gospel-centered, passionate singing. That's why I always
encourage leaders in the church to take time to sing a cappella,
whether it's a line, a verse, or an entire song.

The sound that unites the church should be the sound of voices,
not a particular music style. When people are focused on that sound
and the fact that Jesus has made it possible, style becomes secondary.

Musical Creativity in the Church Has Functional Limits

Here's another implication: musical creativity in the church has functional limits. The church will always be exploring new and different
ways of expressing God's glory and our response to him. But God did
not assign us the task of singing the most radical, cutting-edge, creative music possible. In other words, our personal music collection is
not the best place to begin when thinking about what songs we should
sing on Sunday. We want to pursue a creativity that is undistracting, a
creativity that unites the church around gospel-centered truth rather
than dividing the church over musical innovation.

The Gospel, Not Music, Unites Us

Finally, we must be clear that it is the gospel and not music that unites
us. An increasing number of churches have adopted the practice of
offering different services for different musical tastes. While that deci-
sion can be well intentioned, I believe the long-term effect is to separate families and generations and to imply that we gather together
around our musical preferences, not Jesus Christ.

What does it say to the world when we can't prefer each other long enough to have a meeting? Worshiping God together is just one part of our overheard witness to the world. We're saying that the gospel—not musical styles, preferences, or backgrounds—is what unites us. Ephesians 2:14 says, "For he himself is our peace, who has made us both one and has broken down in his flesh the dividing wall of hostility." He has not only broken down the walls of nationality, race, and class. He has broken down the walls of musical preference.

I don't love the people in our church because we like the same kind of music, because we can all name the same bands, or because we all sing from the same hymnal. I love the people in my church because Jesus has enabled me to love them through his once-and-for-all atoning death.

In the book of Revelation, the host of heaven aren't in unity because of the style of music they are using but because of the focus of their song. We read about it in Revelation 5:10:

And they sang a new song, saying,

> "Worthy are you to take the scroll
>   and to open its seals,
> for you were slain, and by your blood you ransomed people
>   for God
> from every tribe and language and people and nation,
> and you have made them a kingdom and priests to our God,
>   and they shall reign on the earth."

What kind of music do people from every tribe and language and nation and tongue sing? I don't know! God didn't tell us. He didn't include a soundtrack with the Bible (although don't you sometimes wish he had?).

Instead, God has told us what the *focus* of our songs should be: worthy is the Lamb who is slain. The Lamb must always be central to our corporate singing. Why? Because Jesus is the One who has made it possible.

We can tend to think that God accepts our offerings of musical worship because of our skill, efforts, practice, or sincerity. If that were the case, our offerings wouldn't be accepted at all. Harold Best reminds us that all our offerings "are at once humble and exalted by the strong, saving work of Jesus Christ."[8] They're humbled because none of our songs would reach God's ears apart from the song of our Savior. Our song is joined with his song; his glorious, perfect song of praise. What exalts our offerings is that God receives our songs as though Christ himself were singing them. Amazing, isn't it?

There have been times when I've listened to recordings of myself leading worship and thought, "That's horrible. How can God put up with that?" He can because he hears what we do through his Son. Certainly there's a place for skill, practice, and sincerity in our worship. But our faith is not in what we do. It's in what Jesus has accomplished on our behalf and in our place at the cross.

Anticipating the Songs to Come

So, what are we doing in our local churches to promote, encourage, and participate in the kind of corporate singing we see in Revelation? What are we doing to discourage it? Leaders should be faithful to model and instruct the church in the purpose of singing, because we live in a musically addicted culture. We need to teach how music functions in corporate worship so that our singing more and more resembles what we see in the book of Revelation. There, in the context of the new heavens and the new earth, we'll forever lift up undistracted, passionate, unified, Word-centered songs to the one who sits on the throne and to the Lamb who was slain.

In his book *Recalling the Hope of Glory*, Allen Ross reminds us of the value of looking ahead:

> If we even begin to comprehend the risen Christ in all his glory, or faintly hear the heavenly choirs that surround the throne with their anthems of praise, or imagine what life in the presence of the Lord will be like, then we can never again be satisfied with worship as usual. We will always be striving to make our worship fit for glory; and we will always be aware that our efforts, no matter how good and noble, are still of this world and not yet of that one.[9]

What will we experience in *that* world, in the new heavens and new earth? While we won't be singing all the time, I can tell you this: when we do sing, it will be like nothing we've ever experienced.

We'll have clearer minds to take in the glories of God. We'll have new strength to give him the glory he deserves. And we'll have an unlimited time in which to do it, free from any and every influence of sin. Singing will fully and finally serve the purpose for which it was intended.

And until that day we continue to sing—thanking God for old songs that join us with the saints of history, enjoying new songs that enable us to express eternal truth in fresh ways, and anticipating the songs that are yet to come.

The Savior has rescued us that we might sing the song of the redeemed. May we sing it well. May we sing it constantly. May we sing it passionately. May we sing it for his glory and the advancing of his gospel until the time comes when our songs will never end.

PART ONE

A Conve
the Cont

John Piper, Mark Driscoll,
Sinclair Ferguson, and Justin Taylor

The following is an edited transcription of a panel discussion on September 26, 2008, at the Desiring God National Conference, where the messages in this book were originally delivered. Justin Taylor's questions are in bold.

John, was there anything in particular from Sinclair's message that stood out to you as something you need or want to apply personally to your life? What convicted you? And then, Mark, you can answer the same.

Piper: Let's start at the structural level, not the heart level. Homiletically, Sinclair moved from a list of twenty resolutions (setting us up like good legalists) to the gospel through James 1:18. He observed that it's the new birth through the Word (which, of course, is the word of the gospel, as 1 Peter 1:23 makes plain), and then went back to Isaiah to let Isaiah flesh out the Savior role of the content of the Word. That was all very helpful for me. James is not an easy book to preach the gospel from, because it's a sort of wisdom literature, and it alludes to the gospel more than it opens it directly. So at the homiletical, structural level it was exemplary and challenging and helpful and satisfying.

At the heart level it was his emphasis that we want to walk out of a room or an elevator and have either our breath or our accent leave people with questions—"Where's he from?" And that will happen, he said, if we are taking in the Word of God so that it so shapes us, so that what comes out has a Bible accent or a Christ accent. That, I think, will bear fruit in my life.

onvicted that as teachers we're going to be judged strictly
ve had some notable failures, so I found that deeply convict-
helpful. And the solution, he said, is to have Scripture come in
appropriate speech comes out. Personally, I found that very help-
d convicting. Sometimes as a teacher—I think a lot of teachers may
uggle with this—we study so that we can teach, or we study so that we
can learn, or we study so that we can inform others. And it was convicting that I need to have the Scripture saturate my thinking for the sake of
living as a Christian, not just as a Christian teacher. Those are conviction
points I noted and have to pray through. I was helped, I was served, and
I'm sincerely thankful.

**Sinclair, I've never heard the story of how the Lord drew you to himself and
then how he called you to pastoral ministry. Could you tell the story of how
God brought you to the gospel and then to pastoral ministry?**

Ferguson: Well, it's a long story, Justin. But the short-form version of it is
this:

I was brought up in a very small, loving, highly disciplined family without gospel. I think my parents thought they were Christians. But until I was
converted, I have a memory of being at only two religious services with
them. One was my grandmother's funeral when I was seven, and the other
was a rather bizarre service that my mother and father took me to.

I was born in 1948. In the early fifties in Scotland, most parents still
thought that a decent part of a child's upbringing was to send him to Sunday
school, and so I was just sent to the church at the end of the street. It was
very mixed but had some particularly impressive Sunday school teachers,
and I sensed that from the beginning. (Only when I was converted did I
realize why they were so impressive.) One of them said to me, when, I think,
I was about nine, "You should join the Scripture Union," which is a Bible
reading society very well known in the British Commonwealth countries.
(It exists in the United States but not very prominently.) It provided very
simple commentaries on Scripture for nine-year-old boys, fifteen-year-old
boys, twenty-five-year-old people. And so I just started reading the Bible,
and in the next five years I probably missed no more than five days. But
for all those years I thought being a Christian was reading the Bible, saying
my prayers, and helping old ladies across the street or giving them my seat
on the bus. It seems almost incredible to me now that I could have read the
Bible so much and not actually seen Christ in the Bible.

Then when I was fourteen, a number of things happened. There was a
minor awakening in the church, and I began to make connections between
what I'd been reading in the Book and what I was seeing in other people's

lives. While I was reading along, I remember—very vividly—reading the Lord saying, "You search the Scriptures and you think that in them you'll find life, but you won't come to me" [cf. John 5:39–40]. It was just like an illumination. I realized this was exactly where I was. I think it was that which then sent me on this quest for Christ. I then went through a period of about four or five months when I was very deeply convicted of my sin.

And I remember one night I was coming home—I started going to the evening church services as well as the morning services—from church. It was a very frosty, icy Sunday night in January 1963, and I almost lost my balance. Just as I regained my balance there was this man standing there dressed from head to toe in black. He looked at me, and then he glanced down and saw the little Bible in my hand. And he said to me, "Are you saved, son?" I burst into tears. I just couldn't grasp how this total stranger that I bumped into because of the ice could see right through me into what I was longing for.

Then I went to hear the gospel preached from John 8:12: "I am the light of the world. He who follows me will not walk in darkness but of life." That was really the text that clinched my sense that Christ was mine and I was Christ's. So that was when I was fourteen.

Then, within the next eighteen months, I had this very profound sense that God was calling me into the ministry. That was a strange thing for me, because speaking isn't very natural to me. Writing is very natural to me. I was educated to write, not to speak. We almost never spoke in class when I was a boy at school, so it was a great challenge to me how this could possibly be.

The other great challenge was that I knew I would have to go to university in order to become a minister, and I didn't know a single soul in my whole family tree who had ever gone to university. So as far as I was concerned, this was like climbing the Himalayas (in those days there were very few places to go to university in Scotland). But by God's grace I went to university.

By the time I was seventeen I had become absolutely convinced of the absolute infallibility and authority of Scripture. If that was the case, the whole Bible must be preachable. But I didn't know anybody who either believed or practiced that.

In those days there were six universities in Scotland. I was determined I would go to one of the four ancient universities (i.e., one that was five hundred years old). I lived in Glasgow, and I thought it would be good for me to be away from home. People from Glasgow are very prejudiced against Edinburgh, and I shared that prejudice, so I wasn't going to go to university in Edinburgh. I played golf competitively, and therefore I decided it wouldn't be wise to go to St. Andrews because I might be tempted from this calling God had given me. And so I went to Aberdeen, which was about 150 miles away from home. I really thought I was going to the ends of the earth!

My folks had started coming to church and trusted in the Lord, and somebody had said to my dad, "When Sinclair goes to university, tell him to go and hear Willie Still." He was a minister in Aberdeen. And by God's grace that was the best thing I did. He was a most eccentric man; he just lived in the presence of God but in a completely eccentric way. His preaching style was totally eccentric. But he must have preached through the Bible three times in his ministry. The church prayer meeting was the most amazing phenomenon I think I've ever experienced. It was like being taken up in a helicopter, and for two-and-a-half hours on Saturday night this group of ordinary people would just tour the world crying out to God for places I'd never heard of. The stamp that left on me was just phenomenal, absolutely phenomenal.

And there's many years after that, but that's the short part.

John, in Sinclair's message he talked about the twin dangers of speaking too much and speaking too little, and I was thinking about this in terms of controversy. How do you avoid the extremes? There are some who love controversy too much and some who are cowardly about controversy. How do you walk the biblical path in the middle?

Piper: I think Sinclair's first resolution is to *pray for wisdom*, and so that would be the first step. I would say, "Lord, there's no clear statement in the Bible—'Engage in that controversy and don't engage in that one'—so I need extraordinary wisdom."

Second, I think it would relate to *the seriousness of the issue*—the ripple effect on the hurting of people and the dishonoring of God. That's usually defined by how close it is to the gospel. (Not always. The manhood and womanhood issue might not look like it's close to the gospel, but its implications feel pervasive to me. That would be one). So I pray for wisdom and try to discern: if this catches on and succeeds, how many people will be hurt and how much will God be dishonored?

Third, I would ask, *Am I suited for this?* A lot of debates I'm not even touching because I don't know enough to be useful there. And so I consider my own bent, giftedness, time, and location as a pastor. There are some issues where I'm going to have to lean on other scholars because I don't have the time to be as much of an expert in it as you would need to be. So my own situation would be the third criterion.

The fourth thing that comes to my mind is, *Is it burning in me?* When I lie down and get up, is it there?

The fifth would be, *Is it affecting those nearby in my life?* Is this something my son is dealing with, my church is dealing with, my staff is dealing with? If it's that close, you don't have an option anymore. And if you're going to deal with it for one person, you might as well put it on the Web and just multiply your usefulness.

So those would be some of the steps. But really it's the first one, where it's going to boil down to whether or not I should get involved with this and to what degree I should get involved.

Mark, as one involved in a fair bit of controversy, what have you learned from those who have criticized you well and those who have criticized you poorly, both in terms of how best to receive criticism and then how best to give it to others? What has some of the criticism taught you?

Driscoll: I once read a biography on Billy Graham entitled *The Leadership Secrets of Billy Graham*, and it had a really good section in there on how Billy handled critics.[1] I learned a lot from that. He oftentimes turned his "critics into coaches." He would consider what they had to say, and he would prayerfully spend time with God, basically asking, "Is there any truth in this? Even if the tone is bad, if the intent is bad, if the heart is malicious, if the facts are misconstrued, is there anything in here that is of truth that I need to heed?" And then he would meet with his critics. He would actively pursue his most vocal critics in an effort to hear them, to repent or consider anything that was worthwhile, to answer any confusion that they may have. And in so doing, Billy Graham became Billy Graham, a guy who was able to build bridges with a lot of different people who started off as very vocal opponents and critics. I was convicted that, in the providence of God, what is intended for evil could be used for good if there's humility enough to consider and discernment enough not to believe everything that's said.

So, for me, it's continually trying to learn how a critic could become a coach and, in the providence of God, how the critic could be of assistance in helping me to grow.

Also I think it has made me more tender toward those who are criticized. I was watching Sports Center the other night. And they were talking about an NFL quarterback who was injured and basically had had a nervous breakdown, and the team was worried about him because he couldn't handle the pressure and the criticism. Probably for the first time in my life I actually felt like praying for an athlete. So I'm sitting there praying for this athlete, that if he does know Jesus that Jesus would comfort him, and if he doesn't know Jesus that he would meet Jesus so that his identity could be in Christ, not in his performance, and that he would live for God's glory and not for the approval of the fans who criticize him. We live in a world, though, where communication is instant, constant, global, and permanent. That changes everything.

Can you say those four again?

Driscoll: I stole this from Rick Warren.

- *Instant*: communication now goes out immediately. I mean, people are live-blogging as we speak.
- *Constant*: twenty-four hours a day, seven days a week.
- *Global*: once it's out, it's out to the world.
- *Permanent*: once it's out there, it's out there forever.

This changes the dynamics of criticism in a way that preachers and leaders and politicians and athletes didn't have to deal with in the past. In past years if you were upset, you'd write a letter and send it to the newspaper, and they could only print a few. If nobody read it, it was done forever. It's not that way anymore. Now it's instant, constant, global, permanent. It can make you so timid and careful that you really lose your ability to speak with any authority. And when you do make a mistake and sin, as I have, you have to live with that forever. There's a certain sorrow that comes with that, if I'm totally honest. There's a grief, a regret, a conviction, and a hope to do better.

What have you learned from those who have criticized you well?

Driscoll: Proverbs says, "The wounds of a friend are to be trusted much" [cf. Prov. 27:6]. When criticism comes from someone who has *love* for you and *hope* for you, I think those two things define a friend. When they criticize you, it is really helpful. Dr. Piper is that kind of friend. C. J. Mahaney is that kind of friend. They have hope for me and love for me, and so when they criticize me it's not to destroy me; it's to help me. And that's what I think Proverbs is talking about. Others—they don't have hope for you, they don't have love for you. Some of them don't even make time for you. They're just snipers for Christ. They are just always looking for somebody to shoot, and you don't even see it coming. They use words like *discernment* and stuff.

Sinclair, I know that in times of discouragement the Psalter has been particularly sweet for you. Can you share the way in which you use the Psalms to work through dark seasons or through periods of discouragement in your soul?

Ferguson: Somewhere fairly early on in my Christian life I realized that afflictions, in general, and the kind of thing Mark has been speaking about, in particular, have the function not only of correcting me but also of giving me a deeper sensitivity to Christ.

I am not an Old Testament or New Testament scholar. I probably have not thought as much about hermeneutics as other people have. But I think that, by God's grace, I've learned these basic instincts: to think about the Psalter in a series of different dimensions that all will get me to Christ. To me, that is really an absolutely fundamental aspect of the lenses through which I'm trying to look at everything. What is this teaching me *about Christ*? How is this meant to make me *more like Christ*? If I have no idea what's happening in my life, what *patterns* might I see in this teaching that can keep this principle fixed in my mind: there is absolutely nothing that can ever happen to me but that God means to take it and use it and make me more like Christ.

You know, when Mark was speaking, I was thinking about his friends who say, "You are this . . . but you shall be that." That is the Christlike way [John 1:42]. So I think, in all criticism, whether it's true or false, you are able to look for this kernel of divine providence. That means as you respond to it in grace, you can never be the loser from it, because at the end of the day it will shape you.

So at the end of the day the resurrection is the inside of you that Christ has forged bursting outside. One of the things I delight to think about as I see friends who have often been wrongly criticized is to say to myself, *What is it going to look like when Christ shows me what he was doing inside him or her and turns it outside?* So we are living for that day, living for Christ, understanding that the whole of the Christian life involves an ongoing communion with Christ of being conformed to his death in order to be conformed to his resurrection [Phil. 3:10–12].

Those are just lenses that I think you see patterned always in the Psalter and consummately found in Christ and then taught in the New Testament. Those are lenses that I think help to keep me looking at the world and at my own life in a relatively stable way.

Pastor John, Matthew 12:36–37 says, "I tell you, on the day of judgment people will give account for every careless word they speak, for by your words you will be justified, and by your words you will be condemned." If we have to give an account on judgment day for every careless word, how is that not massively discouraging?

Piper: I don't believe that "give account for" here means they become the *ground* of our acceptance with God. I think that because of other things Jesus says, especially to the publican who "went down to his house justified" because he just cried out for mercy, knowing he had failed with his tongue ten thousand times and wouldn't "even lift up his eyes to heaven" [Luke 18:9–14]. Jesus said he's accepted. So my understanding of justification by faith alone apart from the work of the tongue stands.

Having said that, I don't think the bottom will fall out in discouragement. You can be discouraged at one level, but the bottom is not going to fall out. You've got your feet on the rock of the sovereign, free grace of God, purchased by One who never spoke amiss and whose righteousness with his tongue will be counted as the righteousness of my tongue. So that's the basis on which we stand.

Now you have manifested in the New Testament "judgment according to works." And "according to" is not the same as "on the ground of" or the "foundation of" your acceptance. We will be, I believe, rewarded according to the good or bad that we've done with our tongues. And my understanding of how that works is that the reward consists in our greater or lesser capacity to enjoy God and all the benefits of heaven. Jonathan Edwards's analogy is that everybody will be perfectly happy, but some will have bigger cups to fill than others.[2] So we'll all be perfectly happy, and nobody will be living a life of eternal frustration in heaven because they were saved like the thief on the cross—who will have to give an account for his tongue (all he ever did with his tongue except for the last half hour was sin). So my picture of the last day is that there will be tears at that moment of sorrow and regret, and I think the Lord will look at me, and I will just crumple, in one sense, because of how much I've let him down. So in that sense it is discouraging. It's just not decisively, eternally, horribly, suicidally discouraging.

There are passages that apply here, and one of my favorites is in Micah 7 where the prophet says, "When I fall, I will rise and the Lord will execute judgment for me and not against me, even though I am now under the darkness of his disapproval" [cf. Mic. 7:8–9].

My picture is that the filing cabinet for John Piper's life will be pulled out on the last day. Everything's written down—sixty-two years' worth. And the folders will all have grades on them: F, D, C+, maybe here and there a B-. And God will take everything that does not function as an evidence of my new birth, and he'll pull it out and show it to me. I'll be grieved, and he will throw it away. He'll cover it with the blood of Jesus. And he'll take this little, little bundle that's left, like from B- down to C-, and he'll hold it up to the entire universe and say, "This is proof positive he was born again." That's the way I understand the judgment according to works. "Since he's born again, he's united to my Son, and my Son never spoke anything amiss, and therefore, all of John Piper's failures are covered here."

Mark, this glorious doctrine of Christ's substitutionary atonement is being mocked in some quarters, and yet you preach it, and your church continues to grow. How do you counsel people from the cross?

Driscoll: In the book *Death by Love* I retell some stories from people that I pastor and then I write them a letter talking about how Jesus' death on the cross is really the answer for them. The preface to each is on penal substitutionary atonement from a theological perspective, and the letters are very pastoral. So, for example, I write a propitiation chapter to someone who's a convicted pedophile.

I think the most painful for me personally was a very dear woman, a friend. She was raped and always felt dirty and defiled and unclean, and it affected her marriage very negatively. And I write the expiation chapter to her, how Jesus cleanses us from our unrighteousness and how the bride in Revelation gets to wear white, and so does she in Christ. About a third of the women in our church were raped or molested. It's a huge part of our ministry. A growing part of what we do is to try to help them to serve. We're convinced that apart from the cross of Jesus, we have no help to offer anyone. All we're left with then is just *Christus exemplar*: Jesus lived like this; try your best—which is nothing but despairing.

Instead, we teach that Jesus died to give new life, and so we connect the atonement with regeneration. This is what Jesus did so that you might live. All our counseling, all our shepherding, comes out of that. And we are seeing people saved by the hundreds and hundreds and hundreds, upwards of a couple hundred people baptized on certain days just in the last year. I don't take any credit for that, but I'm glad. I'm getting to see people meet Jesus, and I'm getting to see them deal with real issues, sin they've committed, sin that's been committed against them. And it's encouraging.

Those who want to give away the cross want to give away conversion and just be left with a vague spirituality that leaves Jesus as a great example. Whatever religion you're in, you could just give it an effort. And I think that's where a lot of theology is going.

But I see this other resurgence of a love for the Scriptures, a love for Jesus, a love for the cross, a love for very hard doctrines like the wrath of God and substitutionary atonement. And where I see those doctrines being believed and preached, we are seeing churches planted and growing, reaching very young, very pagan, very lost people. So I have good news. I guess the gospel is still powerful!

When I talk to people outside theological circles about these sorts of things and tell them that there are people denying substitutionary atonement, they ask what the alternative is they're putting in its place. How would you

answer that? What is the alternative to substitutionary atonement and the full-bloodied doctrine of biblical atonement? What are they arguing that's different from what you're saying?

Driscoll: One guy put it well: it's *moralistic therapeutic deism.*[3] Moralistic—try to be a good person. Therapeutic—God just gives principles for better living. And deism—he doesn't really regenerate you or live in you by the power of the Holy Spirit. God is sort of far away and intervenes in crisis moments. Other than that, you're pretty much on your own. And I would say that moralistic, therapeutic deism dominates with Oprah, it dominates with a lot of prosperity teachers, it dominates with a lot of psychologized theology. It doesn't work, but it's popular and it pays the bills for some. So I think that's what is in place of substitutionary atonement.

As soon as that's in place of real Christ-centered, Bible-centered, atonement-centered, repentance-centered, regeneration-centered Christianity, then the distinction between who is and who is not a Christian and what is and what is not Christian becomes almost indistinguishable. And in this age of pluralism there's a great thrust to carve out some center like mortality or therapy or spirituality as a unifying center—because Jesus as the center is only unifying for those who repent. For everyone else he is not a unifying center; he's a dividing line. The first mark of a Christian is repentance, turning from that kind of life toward Jesus. So when it's all said and done, those are the only two alternatives: walk toward him or away from him.

Piper: What goes first before the cross is the wrath of God. The only reason you need propitiation is if God's mad at you and will send you to hell. When that goes, you do something else with the cross. Consider Steve Chalke's book where he got in trouble for calling the penal substitution "divine child-abuse."[4] Clearly from that one paragraph he had already abandoned the wrath of God as it's biblically understood. He says—and this is my answer to your question *what's in its place?*—"God keeping his own commandments." God said love your neighbor as you love yourself, and love your enemy. Chalke says sending anyone to hell is clearly not enemy love.

So I think the alternative is universalism and the abandonment of the wrath of God. If you keep central the holiness of God responding in justice to sinners with omnipotent wrath justly meted out in eternal torment, then the cross is understood and gloriously true and helpful.

Ferguson: It strikes me how fragile contemporary Christians are, because we think that the gospel came about ten years ago.

In 1999 there was a fascinating poll in the United Kingdom asking the British public to name the two most significant figures of the previous millennium, from 1000 to 2000. You have some giant human beings in the last thousand years, but the result of the poll was that Nelson Mandela was the most significant man and Princess Diana was the most significant woman! And that really confirmed something I suspected about the great British public—they know almost no history.

There is a kind of a parallel in the church. People who purvey an anti-penal substitution doctrine of Christ don't seem to realize that men did that in the nineteenth century and destroyed the church. They did it in the eighteenth century and destroyed the church. They did it in the seventeenth century and destroyed the church. And they did it in the sixteenth century and destroyed the church. We've really seen it all before, and we know in advance what the fruits will be. It will be the destruction of radical Christianity. It will be the destruction of a radical sense of the forgiveness of sins. It will lead to a commensurate destruction: when you destroy the wrath of God, you absolutely destroy the heights of joy and glory that a Christian may experience in this life. Just a little knowledge of the history of the church would be just such a help to us.

Sinclair, with this new resurgence of younger Reformed evangelicals, we hear a lot about the centrality of the cross but not as much about union with Christ—its importance as a doctrine or its practical effects. Can you say a bit about the importance of union with Christ for our growth and holiness?

Ferguson: I come from a kind of old-style Reformed church—John Knox, John Calvin. I live in South Carolina. I don't even know what emergent or non-emergent is! As a kind of sideline observer I see people becoming the "New Reformed" of our time and people from the "Old Reformed" sometimes jumping on their heads because they don't get it all together instantaneously. And I want to say, "I thought you believed in the sovereignty of God and learned to be patient with people!" So I do think it's true that when people really do come to realize and get back to the centralities—the wrath of God, the penal substitution of Christ, the absolute necessity of regeneration as a sovereign work of God—in the ordinary course of events as people keep processing the Scriptures, then the other pieces eventually get into place.

Calvin was like that. He saw the judgment of God; he saw the necessity of regeneration, the necessity of faith in Christ, but it was quite a while before he began to work through the implications of what it means to believe in union and communion with Christ and to understand that from the moment you become a Christian you are somebody who has died to sin and been raised to newness of life. You are somebody over whose life the dominion of the power of sin has been broken.

You begin to learn to interpret your life in terms of what God says about you because you are united to Christ instead of interpreting the gospel in terms of where you are in your struggle. I need to live the Christian life out of a center of being united to Christ. And, therefore, the whole of the Christian life is stamped with participation in sufferings, "filling up what is lacking in Christ's afflictions" [cf. Col. 1:24]—not in any lack in their atoning significance, nor any lack in Christ at all, but what remains of me being brought to full Christlikeness by participation in the sufferings of Christ. And almost cyclically I then experience participation in the resurrection of Christ until those two realities are consummated when I'm finally delivered not just from the power of sin but from the very presence of sin and then actually physically conformed to the likeness of his glorious resurrection body [Phil. 3:21].

That is a long, slow process. When Peter said there are some things in Paul's letters that are difficult to understand [2 Pet. 3:16], I think maybe he was thinking about passages like Romans 5 and Romans 6. It can take a long, hard look into the notion of union with Christ before, you know, the little grey cells begin to grasp this amazing reality that I'm united to Christ the same way the branches are united to the vine, that this is not some spooky, mystical thing. It is grounded in what he has done. Then, as I realize what he has done, it really does become a mystical (or spiritual) reality for me, and out of that I learn to live the whole of my life in union and communion with Christ.

To me this is just the totally amazing reality of the Christian life: that my union with Christ emerges into a daily communion with Christ. I am so united to him that in everything I am making reference to him. I sometimes think if people could see inside my head they would think I was absolutely off my head and ask the question, "Who is this *other* in his life?"

That would be the blessed reality for every Christian believer if we only just believed the gospel that we believe!

PART TWO

A Conversation with the Contributors

John Piper, Bob Kauflin, Paul Tripp, Daniel Taylor, and Justin Taylor

---

The following is an edited transcription of a panel discussion on September 27, 2008, at the Desiring God National Conference, where the messages in this book were originally delivered. Justin Taylor's questions are in bold.

Bob, you're one of the happiest men that I know. But several years ago you went through a period of intense emotional suffering. I wonder if you would be willing to share a bit about what you went through, how the Lord used his words and the words of others to bring you through it, and what you learned from it.

Kauflin: I helped plant a church in Charlotte, North Carolina, in 1991. I began to feel increasing anxiety at different times when we first planted the church. Then in January of 1994 my wife and I were at a couple's house for dinner, and I cracked. My life fell apart. Mentally I had no connection with what I was doing, no connection with the past, no connection with the future. I didn't know why I existed. These were the thoughts that went through my brain. That began a period of maybe three years where I battled constant hopelessness. I would wake up each morning with this thought: "Your life is completely hopeless," and then I would go from there. It was a struggle just to make it through to each step of the day. The way I made it through was just to think, *What am I going to do next? What will I do? I can make it to there.*

It was characterized by panic attacks. For the first six months I battled thoughts of death. I'd think about an event that was three months away:

Why am I thinking about that? I'm going to be dead by then. I had feelings of tightness in my chest, buzzing and itching on my arms, buzzing on my face. It was a horrible time. And in the midst of that I cried out to God, and I certainly talked to the pastor that I served with and other pastors that I knew—good friends—trying to figure out what in the world was going on with my life.

Five or six children at that time, a fruitful life, a fruitful ministry. And this is what I discovered: although I'd been a Christian for twenty-two years (since 1972) I was driven by a desire to be praised by men. And I wasn't succeeding. When you plant a church, you find out that there are a lot of people who don't agree with you. People who came to plant the church left. All of that assaulted my craving to be admired and praised and loved and worshiped and adored and applauded. God, I believe, just took his hand from me and said, "Okay, you handle this your way." I knew the gospel, but what I didn't know was how great a sinner I was. I thought the gospel I needed was for pretty good people, and that wasn't sufficient to spare me from the utter hopelessness I felt during that time.

I would read Scripture. It didn't make sense to me. It didn't affect me. I remember lying at bed at times just reciting the Lord's Prayer to myself over and over and over, hoping that would help. I couldn't sleep; then at times all I wanted to do was sleep. I remember saying this early on: "God, if you keep me like this for the rest of my life but it means that I will know you better, then keep me like this." That was the hardest prayer I've ever prayed.

During that time I read an abridged version of John Owen's *Sin and Temptation*[1] and Jerry Bridges's *The Discipline of Grace*.[2] About a year into the process I talked to a good friend, Gary Ricucci, whom I am now in a small group with at Covenant Life Church. I said, "Gary, I feel hopeless all the time."

He said, "You know, Bob? I think your problem is that you don't feel hopeless enough."

I don't know what I looked like on the outside, but on the inside I was saying, "You are crazy. You are crazy. I feel hopeless."

He said, "No, if you were hopeless, you would stop trusting in yourself and rely completely on what Jesus Christ accomplished for you."

That was the beginning of the way out. And I remember saying to myself literally hundreds of times—every time these feelings of hopelessness and panic and a desire to ball up in a fetal position would come on me—"I *feel* completely hopeless because I *am* hopeless, but Jesus Christ died for hopeless people, and I'm one of them."

Over time I began to believe that. And today when I tell people that Jesus is a great Savior, I believe it, because I know that he saved me. That's where my joy comes from. My joy comes from knowing that at the very bottom, at the very pit of who I am, it is blackness and sin, but the love and grace of Jesus goes deeper. One of my favorite books has become *The Valley of Vision*,[3] a collection of Puritan prayers, because it so accurately and clearly describes the blackness of our sin and the amazing grace provided in the substitutionary sacrifice of Jesus Christ.

So I am a happy man. I have a lot to be happy about. That was eleven years ago; I have not experienced those kinds of symptoms since. I'm still tempted, obviously, to desire the praise of people. But I don't want it. I learned through that time to truly hate pride and its effects, and I just want to spend the rest of my life learning to hate it more and to love the humility that Jesus Christ died to impart to me. So I'm a grateful man.

Paul, given that both you and your brother Tedd—author of *Shepherding a Child's Heart*—have written so much about biblical Christianity, grace, and the family, a lot of people think that you had an idyllic upbringing and gospel-centered home. I wonder if you could tell your own story about how the Lord brought you to himself.

Tripp: Well, it is a wonderful and amazing experience that Tedd and I are doing what we're doing, and I wake up every morning with a profound sense of privilege. I have these interesting moments. They happen weekend after weekend as I'm out there speaking. Someone will come up and say, "I've heard Tedd. I've heard you. I've read your books. You must have had the most amazing parents." Now, I don't want to be overly critical, but I wonder if we make such conclusions because we don't actually believe in grace, and we think there must be a natural explanation for what we see in people's lives.

So, a bit of my story. My parents both made professions of faith just before I was born. That's why I was given the name Paul David. But I don't know if my dad was a man who ever came to faith. I was telling John that he literally screamed his way into eternity saying, "O God, no! O God, no!" He lived a pretty horrendous double life. But there's one thing my father did that I will be eternally grateful for. I can tell you for sure that ten million years into eternity I will still celebrate this: he read the Bible to us every day. He wasn't a teacher. I don't know if he knew the Lord, but he read the Bible every day. He'd start in Genesis and he'd read through Revelation, and we knew what would happen next: he'd start in Genesis again and he'd read through to Revelation. That left a profound imprint on me. I don't know if I remember all the content that was there, but I knew that this was important. I knew that there was a God and that life had to do with having a relationship with him.

In high school I was invited to a party. There was everything there. I looked at all that was available, all the sin, and what drove me out of that house into the night was the fear of God. I'm very thankful for that.

On the other side, my dad lived a very inconsistent life. My mom was a very troubled lady. Under the guise of God's law, there were many abusive things done. And I see the glorious, gorgeous, mysterious sovereignty of God in all of that, because those two themes of the glory of God and the brokenness of humanity are what drove me toward what would be my life work.

In an act, I think, of a kind of familial desperation, my mom sent my brother Mark and me off to camp for an entire summer. I think she was just emptying the home. She was up against it. We lived in Toledo, Ohio. I remember the long trip to above Scranton, Pennsylvania, to Harmony Heart Camp. We were going to be there the whole summer. My brother Mark was so homesick he ended up living with the director of the camp for the summer. But God placed me, by his grace, in a cabin full of nine-year-old boys with a man who would presume to teach through Romans to nine-year-old boys. His name was also Paul. I want to see him in heaven. I want to kiss that man. By the time we got to Romans 3, I was overcome with the guilt of my sin. I knew that God was my only hope. I was on the third bunk high, and that night I was not able to sleep. They had put us to bed. They had turned the lights off, and I was weeping in my bed. It seemed to me at nine years old that it was profane to just lie there and pray for God's forgiveness. I thought that I ought to be up, so I climbed down trying not to wake anybody and knelt in the middle of that concrete floor and asked for the forgiveness of my Savior and placed myself in the throes of his grace.

I can say these two things: I wouldn't want to live through many of the experiences of growing up again, but I am deeply grateful for them and what God has done for me through them. Who but a God completely sovereign and glorious in grace could do such a thing?

John, I often hear you talk about the "joy and miracle of self-forgetfulness." I wonder if you could explain what you mean by that? If it's a miracle, are there strategies to cultivate it? If you're singing in worship and you become self-conscious of the emotions you're feeling or if your arms are being raised, how do you forget about yourself and focus on the Savior?

Piper: There are things you can do mostly before the moment. But first of all, let me say what it is and where it came from. Humility is an essential reality in the Christian life. Calvin said Christianity is first, humility; second, humility; and third, humility.[4] The more I have thought about it, the more impossible it is to be intentionally humble, because if you succeed in the intention, you're not. In other words, you're aware that you are—and being aware that you are ruins it. Therefore, it's a catch-22 at that moment. Let's say it's a command: "Clothe yourselves, all of you, with humility" [1 Pet. 5:5]. Well, if I succeed in obeying the command, I've done a pretty good thing. So I should feel good about how I succeeded in obeying the command to be humble. So it seems impossible! And I think it is.

That's why I call it a miracle. I think the way you experience humility is by not experiencing it—which is self-forgetfulness. The really humble person is not thinking about himself. He should be thinking about two other things: one is how glorious God is, and the other is how he could help another person, being involved as a servant and being really active. "It's more blessed to give than to receive" [Acts 20:35]. But as soon as I start thinking about that, I'm messing it up. And as soon as I start thinking about how vibrant my worship is, it's gone. So, the miracle of self-forgetfulness is authenticity in a moment of service or worship. That's what I mean.

The way you move toward it, I think, is that you ask for it. I pray that way regularly before I preach. Before others speak, I ask for that gift to be given to them. It's a horrible experience to stand in front of a group, being outside yourself thinking about how you're doing. Because if you're doing well, you'll be really arrogant; and if you're doing poorly, you'll panic: "They're going to leave at any minute, and I'm losing everybody." But there are few experiences in my life more glorious than to wake up at the end of thirty minutes of preaching because I have been so taken with the substance of the text and the person of Christ. So, asking for it is the first step.

Then you need to familiarize yourself with greatness. You get to know something great that draws you out of yourself. It could be nature—clouds, Grand Canyon kind of things. Or it could be God and the Bible. This is why study is so valuable. I have often asked depressed people, "Have you ever read a book of systematic theology?" That might be good therapy. Now, that's really weird for some people, but the whole point is if you could just be drawn out of yourself into something great out there. Or it might be a novel, a story or something. So familiarize yourself with greatness.

Then, I think, in the moment when it happens you can consciously crucify it. If you're worshiping and suddenly you wonder if anybody's watching you—if your hands are up, you wonder if they're watching you, or if you just sang loud and you got the note right, whatever is ruining it at the moment—you can actually say to yourself and to that thought, "Just die," and direct your consciousness back to the substance and to God.

Bob, in your message you had a little line about Screen Dependency Disorder. And you said sometimes, if you don't have the song memorized, you will look at a line and then just look away. I did that a few times after you said that. That's helpful. It's a little thing that increased the authenticity of the moment of engagement with the truth of that line, for whatever reason.

So those are two or three things that, yes, you can do to move toward it. But in the end it's a miracle, because you can't make it happen. It is a gift. Maybe that would be the better word. It's a gift in the moment that you right now are not thinking about yourself.

And how do you recognize the work of the Spirit in your life and the fruit that's being produced and the progress that you've made? For example, I think of Paul—under the inspiration of the Holy Spirit—saying "Be imitators of me" (e.g., 1 Cor. 4:16). So he was being humble in saying, "I want you to look at me, see how I'm doing it, and do it like that." How does that work?

Piper: In this life I think we are cursed with self-awareness, and therefore we *must* use it. I may be wrong here—maybe the pendulum has swung too far—but I do think heaven will be a reality where we are deriving our joy from God awareness, from God's glory. To the degree that we are aware of ourselves and thinking about ourselves, it will be in a way that reflects him better than it does now. Here we must do self-examination. "Examine yourselves to see whether you are in the faith," Paul says [2 Cor. 13:5]. So you do look at yourself. But what you're looking for, I think, among other things, is how much you are thinking about yourself and how little you are thinking about yourself. And if you're thinking about yourself a lot—in other words, if you always live in self-examination and worry and either approval or disapproval of yourself—then you're way too self-preoccupied. That would be a sign that you're in trouble. So one of the things I'm looking for in self-examination is that I don't do too much of it or that I don't get sucked up into standing in front of the mirror all the time trying to figure out whether that's good enough.

But your second question does give me pause. It may be that there are virtues of self-awareness that would keep me from making self-forgetfulness the absolute ideal. So I'll just stop there. And all these folks can figure that out as to whether that's the case or not. But I know for me, the most authentic moments of joy and the most authentic moments of service are the moments where I'm taken out of myself in admiration or out of myself in compassion.

Bob, do you want to follow up on that at all with regard to the aspect of using your body in worship? Lots of people find the idea of raising their hands when they're singing to be very uncomfortable. I think we touched on that briefly, but do you want to say anything more about that?

Kauflin: I think we begin with what God desires and how God desires to be praised and what pleases him. I was having a conversation with Mark Dever a few years ago. Mark Dever is a very formal, wonderful man of God, the pastor of Capitol Hill Baptist Church in Washington, D.C. I was just challenging Mark a little bit, because Mark is not the most physically expressive guy in corporate worship, and yet he is a man of God, theologically brilliant, loves the gospel, loves the church. I said, "Mark, what about this? What if I were to ask you, 'If there is any physical action in Scripture that God says pleases him—raising hands, kneeling, dancing, bowing, shouting—that you've never done, wouldn't it be a good question to ask why not?'" He said, "Yeah, that's a good question." So that's the question. That was it. That's the question that I would ask you if there are certain physical expressions, biblical physical expressions, that you've never done, and say, "Why not?" So that's where I'd start.

In a gathering I think many of us struggle with this self-awareness as though everybody in the room is really looking at us. It's ludicrous. It's crazy. But that's the human heart. That's the desire for our own glory and our own praise. I think it's good just to acknowledge it as sin and confess it and say, "Well, Jesus, that's why you died. You died because I love my own glory. Even now I'm supposed to be praising you. All I can think about is if anybody's looking at me, and I can't shake it. Thank you for dying for this sin."

Then I think of "The Expulsive Power of a New Affection" by Thomas Chalmers, the idea of directing your love somewhere else rather than to yourself. The thing that's been most helpful for me is just to think about the words we're singing. Just to ponder them, to do everything I can to make myself engage with them and to think, "This is true, this is reality, this is why I live, this is why I was created." And you know, when I start doing that, I start moving. I'm not thinking about what I'm doing. When I am thinking about how great the Savior is and what he did for me and how glorious God the Father is and how the Father has sent his Spirit through the Son to live in me, I just have to respond some way. Sometimes that will be kneeling. It's often just lifting my hands, saying, "Thank you" or "I need you." At that point I could care less what people are thinking about me.

It's not my concern, because my third thought is *I want to do with my body whatever makes Jesus Christ look glorious.* If people observe me, I want them to be able to say he knows a great Savior—not an okay Savior, not an average Savior, not a Savior that you can kind of take or leave. I want them to be able to tell from my countenance. Psalm 34:5: "Those who look to him are radiant, and their faces shall never be ashamed." I want them to know from my body that this is what I was created for—to bring him glory. Not just in this setting but as an expression of my life as a whole. To bring glory and honor and praise and worship and adoration to the One who is absolutely worthy. And when I think that way, I think expressiveness just flows more naturally. If it's not something that's normal to us, we may have to do it at home just to get used to it. But I think if we're thinking the right thoughts about the glory of Jesus Christ, physical expression really does come more naturally.

Dan, how would you counsel people to become more creative and to cultivate their imagination in a God-centered way?

Taylor: I think a place to start is simply to value it. You told me in an e-mail about the theology professor you ran into who said, seemingly with a certain amount of pride, that he hadn't read a work of fiction in fifty years. The first thing I would say to him is, "If you're reading theology books you're probably reading a lot of fiction!" And then I'd ask him how he would feel if a pastor said to him with pride, "I've never read a book of theology in fifty years." Would that reflect well on him? I do think it indicates a suspicion of the imagination in the Christian world.

I can remember my grandmother from when I was four years old. I don't know what I said to her, but I remember being in the backseat of a car when I was four years old, and we pulled up to the house. My grandmother opened the door. And as we got out, she looked at me and said, "Don't you story to me." And I realized even as a four-year-old that she was equating *story* with lying. I think there's a lot of that in Christianity—certainly in the circles I grew up in. I grew up with the fundamentalists. (I run into a lot of people who are angry at fundamentalists and are very fundamentalistic about rejecting fundamentalism.) In many important ways I am not a fundamentalist anymore, but I thank God there were people who cared enough to tell me the stories of faith, and so I bless them, and I know there's a lot of truth even maybe mixed up with other things. But my upbringing didn't value the imagination or the creativity.

We also had very plain churches. I know some of the history of why that is, but people would have plain churches who didn't have plain houses. I would wonder why is it that they thought it was a misuse of money to beautify a church but didn't think it's a misuse to make their house look as good as it could possibly look.

So my counsel would be to start with valuing and to start also with certain key doctrines: common grace, and that every human being is made in the image of God (including people who don't acknowledge that). Part of being made in the image of God is having an imagination. My understanding of creation is that God imagined us. That's *ex nihilo*. There was nothing there except God, and God in an act of the imagination imagined the world.

He didn't have anything to make it with. He had to imagine us. So we are the product of imagination. It's one of the aspects of being made in the image of God that we then imagine.

And I've learned tremendous amounts of things from people who do not share my faith commitments and who I think are incredibly wrong about the core meaning of life, and yet they're still made in the image of God. They can still create beautiful things. They still have insight into the human condition. They do write novels. (To tell you the truth, they write better novels than the Christians do. That wasn't always the case, but in the twenty-first century still, although Christians are improving, they write better novels, partly because they don't feel the need to cheat. I think a lot of Christian novelists feel they have to cheat to make it all come out neat and right and happy at the end, and it doesn't always turn out that way.) So I would say cultivate the imagination. Value it—then cultivate it.

How do you cultivate anything but by putting yourself in the presence of it? How do you cultivate a relationship with God but by being in the presence of God in all the many different ways that you can be in God's presence? It's the same with the imagination. Go to the great cathedrals and stand in awe. See the great paintings. Hear the great music. Read the great books. Look at nature, which is, again, God's imagination expressing itself in an infinite number of ways.

Then realize this isn't just what other people have. God gave *me* an imagination, too. Everybody has a certain level of creativity and imagination, but some people have extraordinary levels of it. And what God has called them to do is to use that imagination and creativity in wonderful ways. Don't deny that and don't listen to other people who deny it, and find a way that you're supposed to express it. Use it to the fullest to the glory of God.

Piper: May I make an observation and have Dan respond to it? Back to Justin's question about self-forgetfulness: our children are born proud and sinful, but almost no children express that in terms of self-awareness. Children *learn* to be embarrassed. They learn self-preoccupation—which is a kind of mature adolescent sin that we end up keeping. And it seems to me that one of the healthiest things that guards a kid from that is stories. Anybody can tell a three-year-old a riveting story—just tell him about the day or something! Almost no child or adult being told a riveting story is thinking about himself at the moment. He's drawn out of himself and into the story. It's good mental health.

Our church is located two blocks from a major mental health institution. One of the things that all the folks there have in common—and we love them to death and they come and do funny things at our church and some of them we know really well—is that they're all wrapped up in themselves. All mentally ill people are consumed with themselves. They don't connect right with what other people are praying. They don't understand what's going on in the situation. Everything is just in their minds, swirling around with guilt or fear or panic or whatever. So that's the worst. By and large they are all schizophrenic and on medication. But *all* of us are that way a little bit. And so, to me, mental health is very largely finding out how not to be that way. So any thoughts, Dan, about how story works?

Taylor: Yeah, about thirty-six hours worth! There's no question that stories for children form their moral imagination. Lots of people have commented on this, including C. S. Lewis and secular psychologists like Bruno Bettelheim. Children see in stories that we live in a world where what you do matters, and that there is real good and evil. And they know that. Children's stories are simple, but they're not naïve. They're profoundly true. And that's why adults often like reading to their grandkids. They're reading for themselves as well. So stories begin to form your moral imagination. I personally believe that's true of stories that are not explicitly Christian as well as those that are. *The Lord of the Rings* is a wonderful moral myth that had profound influences on me as an adolescent and made me see that there's good in the world and there's evil in the world, and that I want to be on the side of the good guys. Not because I think the good guys are always winning in the world, because they often aren't. But I just felt the moral force of the story: *I want good to triumph here and I don't want evil to triumph, and I've got to do something.* Stories call out of us the best that God put in us.

This includes compassion. Because what is compassion? Compassion means to suffer with. *Com* means with; *passion* is pain or suffering. If you have compassion, you suffer with someone else. You put yourself in their story—and that takes the imagination. I have to imagine what it's like to be you and to be in need. It draws out of me what is necessary to break out of self-consciousness and solipsistic pure interest only in myself in order to put myself in someone else's shoes.

So I think story or the imagination is at the core of morality, the core of our moral natures. And of course that's the ultimate story. That's the greatest story ever told—that God had compassion for us. What did he do? He joined our story in a physical way. He started our story. He initiated it. But from the foundations he knew that at some point in history and in time he was going to radically join with his creation. And that's called the incarnation.

I think all great artists take good and evil seriously, even if they don't know where it came from. And if they don't take it seriously, then they're not great artists. No great work of literature or art is produced by someone who doesn't take evil and good seriously. So we can learn from those people who haven't put it all together, who don't know or haven't accepted that God has incarnated himself. God still made them, and God has given them at least limited insights into the human condition. So I love any story that brings out of me what God intended from me.

I know that all four of you enjoy and practice art—Dan with literature, John with poetry, Bob with songwriting, Paul with painting. Paul, could you talk about the role that art has had for you in the pursuit of holiness and the glory of God?

Tripp: I love Isaiah: "Holy, holy, holy is the LORD of hosts; the whole earth is full of his glory" [6:3]. We live in the middle of this awesome glory display, but we have this perverse ability to look at the created world and not see the glory of God. If you can look at your world and not see the glory of God, then you're a profoundly disadvantaged human being, because you're wired for glory. If you don't see the glory of God, then you'll see glory where glory can't be found. So that really is the mission of my life: to give people eyes to see the glory of God.

I would argue that the glory of God in creation is so deep that all the elements of creation have glory. Shape has glory. Texture has glory. Light has glory. Color has glory. If you would take a piece of bark off a tree, you don't just have this flat piece of brown bark; you have this multi-layered, multi-textured glory. And you don't have just one shade of brown; you have four hundred shades of brown intersecting and coursing around. It's just a glorious thing.

I was by a pond. I picked up the feather of a bird. I don't know why I picked it up. It looked white. And I had a white shirt on. And when I put it against my white cuff it was gorgeously striped with grey coursing into black. And I thought, "What an awesome God! How many birds are there? And each one of these feathers has been painted with this kind of artistry!" My knees were getting weak. And it was just a feather!

And so what I like to do is to take apart the elements that are glorious and assemble them again. My paintings would be considered abstract. I think there's a mistake in the church that we named "Christian art" as being only photorealism. I'm concerned with the dynamic of visual lethargy in people's lives—that once you've seen the tree ten times, you quit looking. It's like when you drive to work you don't see the sights anymore because you've done it so many times. So I want to yank people out of their lethargy. I want to take the elements out of their setting and assemble them again with the hope that people would re-experience the glory of those elements afresh and anew.

Bob, you have the gift of encouragement in spades. How do you give words of encouragement in a way that's not flattering of other people? And how do you receive it in a way that's not prideful?

Kauflin: Well, I have to say that I've been privileged to have an example of a world-class encourager. I've known him for thirty years, and that's C. J. Mahaney. So just by being around someone like that I see how poor of an encourager I am, and that motivates me to want to do better.

I think encouragement begins in the gospel. It's all gospel, isn't it? It begins by recognizing what God has done for us in Christ and what a gift we have, that our sins are forgiven. Sometimes I think to myself that if I found out I had cancer tonight and then had a horrible, painful, extended season and then died, I would still have reason to joyfully praise God forever for forgiving my sins. So I want to see everything as a gift.

And then encouragement comes from just seeing the people around me and realizing all the gifts that God has given people and all the gifts that I receive because I happen to be around them. So it's recognizing those gifts. I guess the encouragement comes in the commitment to say something, to be aware. Because I think flattery is when we're really encouraging someone else so that we'll be encouraged. We encourage people so as to look good ourselves. That doesn't please the Lord. It doesn't bless the person. I want to encourage people because I'm truly grateful for what they've done. I'm truly grateful for who they are, and I carry that with me, and I just want them to know. I want to live my life like that because it helps in that self-forgetting. If I'm always looking around in a room for who I can encourage, that's a wonderful antidote to self-glorification. I'm just thinking of all the good things in the people around me.

As far as receiving encouragement, well, if you're aware of your sinfulness and how much you've been forgiven, you're aware that anything that someone sees in you is a result of the grace of God at work. It's his work. The fact that you've been able to do it is his grace. The fact that the person perceived it and it benefited them is his grace. The fact that it bore any fruit is his grace. It's all for his glory. So when someone encourages me, I'm as amazed as they are that God did something through me. How does that happen? I don't know. But I'm glad it does, and all of us should have that perspective. God has given us—every one of us—gifts that he uses to affect other people.

When someone says "thank you" for whatever, we can say, "Oh, you're welcome. It's amazing, isn't it? But God is so good. He's so kind," and then transfer the glory to him: "Lord, it is because of you that this person even came up." Also, when people encourage me, I thank them for taking the time to encourage. They didn't have to do that. So those are some of the things that I do.

Piper: Underneath all of that, and it shouldn't go without being said, is when you ask questions like that or anybody else does, the question can sound like you're asking for tips—tips on how not to flatter and tips on how not to feel proud. And there are some. But the real issue is, how does a person develop through Scripture, meditation, and reading a worldview with wrath, holiness, judgment, atonement, propitiation, forgiveness, justification? It's a massive place to be where the identification of a good thing in you has meaning other than building him up in his ego. But a tip won't work there. The only thing that works is a worldview that says, "I'm damned, I'm on my way to hell, I am inveterately proud, I am saved by grace." That's the worldview in which something can come, and it's not three tips that protect me. It's this massive place you stay, on this world you're enveloped in, of how to see everything.

Kauflin: Yeah, that's exactly what I was thinking, but I just didn't have time to say it! I didn't want to hog all the time! It is absolutely true. And those things that I share are things that can help move me along, that can address those tendencies toward self-glorification. But John is absolutely right. *Christ is our life.* Colossians 3: "When Christ who is your life appears, then you also will appear with him in glory" [v. 4]. I grow in graces and grace. We grow in grace because Christ has more of our life.

I just want to affirm that and say absolutely that's what it means to live a gospel-centered life. Everything has to do with the glorious God becoming man to redeem a people for himself for his glory and saving us from eternal wrath and eternal condemnation and giving us the expectation and anticipation of eternal joy in his presence. We have it so good. So, then, things like receiving and giving encouragement are just the overflow.

Notes

Introduction

1. The title of a work by Francis Schaeffer, first published in 1972.

2. Jesus frequently refers to who he is and what he says as a package deal: "me and my words," e.g., Mark 8:38; Luke 6:47; John 12:48; 14:24.

3. Graeme Goldsworthy, *Preaching the Whole Bible as Christian Scripture* (Grand Rapids, MI: Eerdmans, 2000), 83–84.

4. I am indebted to Tim Keller for this fourfold way of thinking about applying the gospel.

5. I'm thankful to Vern Poythress for drawing these contrast proverbs to my attention; see Vern S. Poythress, *In the Beginning Was the Word: Language—A God-Centered Approach* (Wheaton, IL: Crossway, 2009).

Chapter 2: The Bit, the Bridle, and the Blessing

1. The author does not identify himself beyond revealing that he is "James" (1:1). The view of the earliest church tradition is that this is James the (half-) brother of the Lord, and this is certainly in accord with what evidence of authorship there is in the letter, and of what we know of James.

2. Some scholars take "body" here to refer to the church, arguing that this makes sense of the context (teachers), and also of the reference to "members" in 4:1 (see ESV footnote translation) understood not as physical members but as church members. For a judicious assessment, see Dan G. McCartney, *James*, BECNT (Grand Rapids, MI: Baker Academic, 2009) on 3:1–12. I am grateful to Professor McCartney for allowing me to see a prepublication version of his exegesis.

3. Cf. one of the clearest illustrations of this in Colossians 3:1–17; note the exhortations in v. 5 ("Put to death therefore . . . ") and v. 12 ("Put on then . . . ").

4. Bruce K. Waltke, *The Book of Proverbs: Chapters 1–15*, NICOT (Grand Rapids, MI: Eerdmans, 2004), 102.

5. Dr. McCartney reports that it continued to be thus used through 1996 and beyond. *Op. cit.*, at discussion of James 3:6, n. 20.

6. Cited from Sereno E. Dwight's *Memoirs of Jonathan Edwards* in *The Works of Jonathan Edwards*, 2 vols., edited and corrected by E. Hickman; 1834 (repr. Edinburgh; Carlisle: Banner of Truth, 1974), 1:*xxi–xxii.*

7. D. M. Lloyd-Jones, *Romans, Exposition of Chapters 3:20–4:25, Atonement and Justification*, (Edinburgh; Carlisle: Banner of Truth, 1970), 19. (Although not an exposition of the first section in Romans, this was the first volume to appear in print.)

8. From Luther's 1522 preface (to the New Testament), cited from *Martin Luther, Selections from his Writings*, ed. John Dillenberger (New York: Doubleday, 1962), 19. It should be remembered that Luther's *Ninety-five Theses* published only five years before in 1517 had radically deconstructed the authority of a church that had, for all practical purposes, claimed to be the judge of what should be in the canon of Holy Scripture. With the removal of the church's authority for what they believed, the early reformers found themselves in the unenviable situation of having to reconstruct orthodox Christianity. That included making decisions about the most basic issues such as the contents of the canon. To his credit, Luther admitted that the judgment of one man cannot be treated as if it were infallible. Later experience with antinomianism would clarify his thinking on the importance and value of James's perspective.

9. Cf. J. A. Motyer, *The Prophecy of Isaiah* (Downers Grove, IL: InterVarsity, 1993), 77.

10. The translation "the new world" (ESV) is a rendering of the Greek *palingenesis*, which elsewhere is translated "regeneration." The present renewal of regeneration is best seen as a present participation in the final, cosmic transformation that will take place at the return of Christ.

Chapter 3: Is There Christian Eloquence?

1. B. B. Warfield, "Calvin and the Bible," in *Selected Shorter Writings: Benjamin B. Warfield*, 2 vols., ed. John E. Meeter (Phillipsburg, NJ: Presbyterian and Reformed, 1970), 1:398. Originally from *The Presbyterian* (June 30, 1909): 7–8.

2. John Donne, *The Sermons of John Donne*, ed. George R. Potter and Evelyn M. Simpson, 10 vols. (Berkeley: University of California Press, 1953–1962), 6:55.

3. Martin Luther, *A Commentary on St. Paul's Epistle to the Galatians* (Westwood, NJ: Fleming H. Revell, 1953), 369–70.

4. Harry Stout, *The Divine Dramatist: George Whitefield and the Rise of Modern Evangelicalism* (Grand Rapids, MI: Eerdmans, 1991), 104, emphasis added.

5. Cited from Sereno E. Dwight's *Memoirs of Jonathan Edwards* in *The Works of Jonathan Edwards*, 2 vols., edited and corrected by E. Hickman; 1834 (repr. Edinburgh; Carlisle: Banner of Truth, 1974), 1:*cxc*.

6. Quoted in John Stott, *Between Two Worlds: The Art of Preaching in the Twentieth Century* (Grand Rapids, MI: Eerdmans, 1982), 325.

7. Denis Donoghue, *On Eloquence* (New Haven, CT: Yale University Press, 2008), 3.

8. Ibid., 148.

9. E. M. Cioran, *The Temptation to Exist*, trans. Richard Howard (Chicago: Quadrangle, 1968), 126–27, quoted in Donoghue, *On Eloquence*, 136, emphasis added.

10. "The most forceful rejection of eloquence I am aware of is Christ's: 'Get thee behind me, Satan'" (Donoghue, *On Eloquence*, 143).

11. John Wilson, "Stranger in a Strange Land: On Eloquence," www.christianity-today.com/bc/2008/001/9.9.html (accessed Sept. 29, 2008).

12. "The wise, the well born and the powerful epitomized the class from which the sophists came and which the latter helped perpetuate through an elitist educational system which emphasized the art of rhetoric. Given the great sin of the sophistic movement was its boasting. . . . Paul made the Jeremiah prohibition against boasting about wisdom, status and achievement a primary text in this critique of the Corinthian sophistic movement." Bruce Winter, *Philo and Paul among the Sophists: Alexandrian and Corinthian Responses to a Julio-Claudian Movement*, 2nd ed. (Grand Rapids, MI: Eerdmans, 2002), 253–54.

13. E.g., 1 Corinthians 1:25 is eloquent for its conscious shock value because it refers positively to "the foolishness of God" and "the weakness of God."

14. "There are . . . forty-two references to 'sophist' (*sophistes*) in Philo, apart from fifty-two references to cognates, and numerous comments on the sophistic movement." Winter, *Philo and Paul*, 7. "There can be no doubt . . . that sophists and their students were prominent in Corinth and played an important role in the life of the city." Ibid., 140.

15. Winter, *Philo and Paul*, 7–9, gives six sources for our knowledge of the Sophist movement in Corinth.

16. Ibid., 141.

17. Ibid., 144 n. 16.

18. Ibid., 253.

19. "The great sin of the sophistic movement was its boasting." Ibid.

20. To further explore the Bible's literary elements, see Leland Ryken, *Words of Delight: A Literary Introduction to the Bible*, 2nd ed. (Grand Rapids, MI: Baker Academic, 1993).

21. Stout, *The Divine Dramatist*, 1991), 228.

22. Ibid.

Chapter 4: How Sharp the Edge?

1. Martin Luther, *What Luther Says: An Anthology*, vol. 1, comp. Ewald M. Plass (St. Louis: Concordia, 1959), entry no. 3360, p. 1056.

2. Ibid., entry no. 3351, p. 1053.

3. Douglas Wilson, *A Serrated Edge: A Brief Defense of Biblical Satire and Trinitarian Skylarking* (Moscow, ID: Canon Press, 2003), 60.

4. D. A. Carson, "Matthew 23:1," *New Bible Commentary: 21st Century Edition*, 4th ed. (Downers Grove, IL: InterVarsity, 1994).

5. E. Gordon Rupp, *Righteousness of God: Luther Studies* (London: Hodder and Stoughton, 1953), 13.

6. Luther, *What Luther Says*, vol. 1, entry no. 3363, p. 1057.

7. Ibid., entry no. 3367, p. 1058.

8. Martin Luther, *The Table-Talk of Martin Luther*, trans. William Hazlitt, no. 667. http://www.reformed.org/master/index.html?mainframe=/documents/Table_talk/table_talk_5.html#Heading30 (accessed September 24, 2008).

9. Luther, *The Table-Talk of Martin Luther*, no. 668.

10. Luther, *What Luther Says*, entry no. 74, p. 27.

11. Charles H. Spurgeon, *Eccentric Preachers* (Salem: Schmul, 1984), 75–76, quoted in Wilson, *A Serrated Edge*, 83.

12. Charles Haddon Spurgeon, "The Uses of Anecdotes and Illustrations," in *Lectures to My Students* (Grand Rapids, MI: Zondervan, 1954), 389.

13. Roland Bainton, *Here I Stand: A Life of Martin Luther* (New York: Meridian, 1995), 232–33.

14. Luther, *What Luther Says*, entry no. 3372, p. 1059.

15. Ibid., entry no. 3371, p. 1059.

16. Ibid., entry no. 3375, p. 1060.

17. "Satire," in *Dictionary of Biblical Imagery*, ed. Leland Ryken, James C. Wilhoit, and Tremper Longman III (Downers Grove, IL: InterVarsity, 1998), 762.

18. Wilson, *A Serrated Edge*, 53.

19. Luther, *What Luther Says*, entry no. 3366, p. 1058.

20. G. K. Chesterton, *Orthodoxy* (Stilwell, KS: Digireads, 2005), 97.

21. Elton Trueblood, *The Humor of Christ* (New York: Harper and Row, 1964), 10.

22. Ibid., 15.

23. Wilson, *A Serrated Edge*, 90–91.

24. H. D. M. Spence-Jones, ed., *The Pulpit Commentary: Isaiah*, vol. 2 (Bellingham, WA: Logos Research Systems, 2004), 460.

25. Wallace has extensive experience and expertise on Greek lexicography. He has taught Greek and New Testament courses at the graduate school level since 1979. He has a PhD from Dallas Theological Seminary and is currently professor of New Testament studies at his alma mater. His *Greek Grammar Beyond the Basics: An Exegetical Syntax of the New Testament* has become a standard textbook in colleges and seminaries. He is the senior New Testament editor of the NET Bible. Wallace is also the executive director for the Center for the Study of New Testament Manuscripts.

26. Daniel B. Wallace, "A Brief Word Study on Skuvbalon," Bible.org, http://www.bible.org/page.php?page_id=5318.

Chapter 5: Story-shaped Faith

1. Scripture references in this chapter are the author's translation.

2. Alasdair MacIntyre, *After Virtue* (South Bend, IN: University of Notre Dame Press, 1981, 1984), 216.

Chapter 6: Words of Wonder

1. Luther wrote, "Music is a beautiful and glorious gift of God and close to theology. I would not give up what little I know about music for something else which I might have in greater abundance." Cited in Walter Buszin, "Luther on Music," *The Musical Quarterly* 32, no. 1 (1946): 85.

2.   Luther, "Preface to Georg Rhau's Symphoniae iucundae," *LW* 53, cited by Buszin.

3.   Augustine, *Confessions*, XXXIII.50.

4.   Oliver Sacks, *Musicophilia: Tales of Music and the Brain* (New York: Alfred A. Knopf, 2007), 158.

5.   Mark Noll, "We Are What We Sing," *Christianity Today*, July 12, 1999, 37.

6.   Jonathan Edwards, *Religious Affections*, cited in Sam Storms, *Signs of the Spirit: An Interpretation of Jonathan Edwards's* Religious Affections (Wheaton, IL: Crossway, 2007), 53.

7.   John Wesley, Preface to *Select Hymns* (1761).

8.   Harold M. Best, *Music through the Eyes of Faith* (San Francisco: HarperOne, 1993), 156.

9.   Allen P. Ross, *Recalling the Hope of Glory* (Grand Rapids, MI: Kregel, 2006), 474.

Conversation with the Contributors, Part 1

1.   Harold Myra and Marshall Shelley, *The Leadership Secrets of Billy Graham* (Grand Rapids, MI: Zondervan, 2005), 79–90. The reference to "turn critics into coaches" is on p. 84.

2.   Jonathan Edwards, "Sermon VIII" (on Romans 2:10), in *The Works of Jonathan Edwards*, 2 vols., edited and corrected by E. Hickman; 1834 (repr. Edinburgh; Carlisle: Banner of Truth, 1974), 2:902.

3.   Christian Smith and Melinda Lundquist Denton, *Soul Searching: The Religious and Spiritual Lives of American Teenagers* (New York: Oxford University Press, 2005).

4.   Steve Chalke and Alan Mann, *The Lost Message of Jesus* (Grand Rapids, MI: Zondervan, 2003), 182–83.

Conversation with the Contributors, Part 2

1.   John Owen, *Sin and Temptation*, ed. James M. Houston (Minneapolis: Bethany House, 1996).

2.   Jerry Bridges, *The Discipline of Grace* (Colorado Springs: NavPress, 1994).

3.   Arthur G. Bennett, ed., *Valley of Vision* (Carlisle, UK: Banner of Truth, 1975).

4.   John Calvin is citing Augustine, who wrote, "Should any one interrogate me concerning the rules of the Christian religion, the first, second, and third, I would always reply, Humility." *Institutes* 2.2.11.

Subject Index

Ambrosius, 95
Anderson, Scott, 13
Augustine, 123, 166

Bainton, Roland H., 94, 165
Bennett, Arthur G., 166
Best, Harold M., 133–34, 166
Bettelheim, Bruno, 158
Bloom, Jon, 13
Bobbitt, Lorena, 90
Bridges, Jerry, 150, 166
Brownback, Lydia, 13
Bunyan, John, 7, 48
Buszin, Walter, 165, 166

Calvin, John, 25, 68, 69, 76,
    147, 152, 163, 166
Carson, D. A., 87–88, 164
Chalke, Steve, 146, 166
Chalmers, Thomas, 155
Chesterton, G. K., 97, 165
Cicero, 69
Cioran, E. M., 71, 163
Cyril, 95

Demosthenes, 69
Denney, James, 70–71
Dennis, Lane, 13

Denton, Melinda Lundquist,
    166
Dever, Mark, 11, 155
Diana, Princess of Wales, 147
Dillenberger, John, 163
Donne, John, 68, 69, 76, 163
Donoghue, Denis, 71–73, 163
Driscoll, Grace, 11
Driscoll, Mark, 11, 20, 81–104,
    137–48
Dwight, Sereno E., 162, 163

Edwards, Jonathan, 52, 56, 69,
    70, 129, 144, 166
Erasmus, Disiderius, 92

Fee, Gordon, 126
Ferguson, Dorothy, 11
Ferguson, Sinclair B., 11, 19,
    45–46, 137–48
Fisher, Allan, 13
Franklin, Benjamin, 69, 78

Goldsworthy, Graeme, 162
Graham, Billy, 141, 166

Hazlitt, William, 164
Hemingway, Ernest, 117

Heston, Charleton, 106, 109
Hickman, E., 162, 163, 166
Hilton, Paris, 85
Horace, 96
Houston, James M., 166
Howard, Thomas, 117

Juvenal, 96

Kapic, Kelly, 12
Kauflin, Bob, 11, 20, 121–35, 149–61
Kauflin, Julie, 11
Keller, Tim, 162
Knox, John, 147

Lewis, C. S., 158
Lloyd-Jones, D. Martyn, 53, 162
Longman III, Tremper, 165
Luther, Martin, 60, 68–69, 76, 87, 91, 94–95, 96, 101, 121–22, 163, 164, 165, 166

MacIntyre, Alasdair, 116, 165
Mahaney, C. J., 142, 160
Mandela, Nelson, 147
Mann, Alan, 166
Mathis, David, 13
McCartney, Dan G., 162
McGraw, Phil, 89
M'Cheyne, Robert Murray, 52
Meeter, John E., 163
Motyer, J. A., 163
Myra, Harold, 166

Noll, Mark, 126, 166

Owen, John, 12, 150, 166

Philo, 164
Piper, John, 11–12, 19, 67–80, 137–48, 149–61
Piper, Noël, 12
Plass, Ewald M., 164
Potter, George R., 163
Poythress, Vern, 162

Rhau, Georg, 166
Ricucci, Gary, 150
Robinson, Edward G., 106
Ross, Allen P., 134, 166
Rupp, E. Gordon, 91, 164
Ryken, Leland, 164, 165

Sacks, Oliver, 124, 166
Schaeffer, Francis, 162
Shelley Marshall, 166
Simpson Evelyn M., 163
Smith, Christian, 166
Solon, 92
Spence-Jones, H. D. M., 165
Spurgeon, Charles Haddon, 94, 165
Steinbach, Carol, 13
Still, Willie, 140
Storms, Sam, 166
Stott, John, 163
Stout, Harry, 78, 163, 164

Taylor, Daniel, 12, 20, 105–20, 149–61
Taylor, Jayne, 12
Taylor, Justin, 12, 15, 137–48, 149–61

Taylor, Lea, 12
Teresa of Avila, St., 119–20
Tripp, Darnay, 27
Tripp, Luella, 12, 26, 27, 28, 31, 33–34, 38
Tripp, Mark, 30, 152
Tripp, Paul David, 12, 19, 23–44, 149–61
Tripp, Tedd, 151
Trueblood, Elton, 165

Wallace, Daniel B., 99, 165
Waltke, Bruce, 49, 162
Warfield, Benjamin B., 163
Warren, Rick, 142

Wesley, Charles, 126
Wesley, John, 126, 129, 166
Whitefield, George, 69, 70, 78, 163
Wilhoit, James C., 165
Wilson, Douglas, 87, 96, 98, 164, 165
Wilson, John, 163
Winfrey, Oprah, 99, 146
Winter, Bruce, 73, 74, 164

Zwingli, Ulrich 123

Scripture Index

Genesis

Book of	151
1–3	15
1:1	105, 113
Chap. 3	51
11:7	95

Exodus

20:1–17	110

Deuteronomy

4:31	111
31:21	125
32:1–3	21

Joshua

4:6–7	107
4:24	108

1 Samuel

16:23	127

2 Samuel

11–12	113–115
12:1–4	114

1 Kings

18:27	96

Job

1:1	105
1:7	51
2:2	51
31:1ff	55–56

Psalms

Book of	122, 142–143
Chap. 1	96
2:4	96
5:9	51
19:1	79
19:4–5	79
22:16	94
22:20	94
22:22	122
33:2–3	132
33:6	81
34:5	155
47:6	122
51:10	63
51:13–15	63
59:8	96
81:2	132
96:1–2	122
102:18	112
119	79
147:1	124
150	132

Proverbs

Book of	18, 24, 46, 142
1:26	96
4:23–24	56
6:16–17	103
8:13	103
10:32	18
11:22	83
12:13–19	104
12:18	18
13:1	18
13:3	18
13:10	18
13:18	18
14:3	18
14:25	18
15:1	18
15:4	49
15:23	76
16:5	103

16:18	103
19:11	93
19:24	86
22:13	86
25:11	76
26:7	77
27:6	142

Ecclesiastes

3:8	93

Isaiah

Book of	137, 163, 165
1–5	60
3:16–24	84
5:8	60
5:11	60
5:18	60
5:20	60
5:21	60
5:22	60
5:25	60
5:26–30	60
Chap. 6	60–61
6:3	159
6:5	61
42:2–3	63
44:15–17	96
50:4–6	64
53:7	65
56:10–11	93
64:6	99

Jeremiah

Book of	164

Lamentations

Book of	86

Ezekiel

16:25–27	85
22:27	86
23:18–21	85
Chap. 34	82

Joel

1:3	108

Amos   95

4:1	85
6:4–6	85

Micah

7:8–9	144

Zephaniah

3:3	86
3:17	122

Malachi

4:2	79

Matthew

5:21–22	51
6:5	98
6:7	16–17
6:9–13	150
6:16	98
7:3	97
7:6	83
7:15	86
7:24–26	17
8:8	16
8:16	16
8:33	163
10:16	86
11:6	98
11:17	127
12:19–20	63
12:34	48, 49
12:36–37	17, 143
15:6	17
15:12	98
15:18	17
15:18–19	49
16:23	163
17:33	91
19:24	97
19:28	62
22:15	17
Chap. 23	87, 89, 90
23:1	164
23:3–33	88–89
23:13	91
23:23	98
24:35	16
26:30	122
26:41	77

Mark

2:2	16
3:21	47
8:38	162
10:24	16
12:34	78

Luke

2:1	105
4:4	16
4:22	16
4:32	16
6:43–45	29
6:45	29
6:47	162
9:26	16
10:3	86
10:30	105
11:28	16
15:11–32	83
19:48	16
18:9–14	144

John

Chap. 1	16
1:6	105
1:14	81
1:42	143
3:3	62
Chap. 4	82
5:24	16
5:39–40	139
6:63	16
6:68	13, 16
8:11	110
8:12	139
8:31	16
8:37	17
8:43	17
8:44	91
8:47	16
8:52	16
8:55	16
10:11	82
10:14	82
12:48	162
14:24	17, 162
15:7	16
17:8	16
17:17	55

Acts

13:10	91, 92
17:30	89
18:24	73
20:29	86
20:35	153
27:37	49

Romans

Book of	152
Chap. 3	152
3:13	51
3:19	53
3:20–4:25	162
Chap. 5	148
Chap. 6	148
11:22	81
Chap. 14	82
14:15	52

1 Corinthians

Book of	19, 73–76
1:10–12	73
1:26–29	75
1:30–31	75–76
1:17	19, 67, 72, 74, 76
1:18	74
1:20	74
1:25	164
2:1	19, 67–68, 72
2:1–2	75, 76
4:16	154
8:11	52
15:7	47

2 Corinthians

5:15	32–33
10:10	73
11:13	91
13:5	154

Galatians

Book of	163
4:6	68
5:15	43, 94
5:11–14	90
5:13–15	35–37

Ephesians

2:14	133
4:29–32	82
5:18–19	122–123
5:19	122

Philippians

3:2	86, 91, 94
3:8	99
3:10–12	143
3:21	148

Colossians

1:16	72
1:24	148
1:28–29	46
2:8	86
2:18	86
3:1–17	162
3:4	161
3:5	162
3:12	162
3:16	16, 122, 126, 127
3:16–17	64
3:17	77
4:3	101

1 Thessalonians

5:25	101

2 Thessalonians

3:1	101

1 Timothy

1:3–7	86–87
1:19	87
1:19–20	91
4:1–2	87
4:7	87
5:20	83
6:3–5	87

2 Timothy

2:14–18	87
2:17–18	91
2:23	87
3:16	86
4:2	46, 83
4:14	91

Titus

1:9	83
1:10–14	87
1:13	83
2:15	83

Hebrews

1:3	15
2:12	122
4:12	54
11:8	116

James

Book of	46
1:1	162

1:5	101
1:5–8	56
1:8	54
1:9–10	56
1:13	56–57
1:18	62, 137
1:19	57
1:22–25	48
1:26	48
2:1	60
2:1–4	57
2:12	57
2:15–16	57
2:19	111–112
3:1	138
3:1–12	19, 45–66
3:3–5	48
3:14	57
4:1	58, 162
4:6	103
4:11	58
4:13	58
4:15	58
5:9	58
5:12	58
5:13	59
5:14	59
5:16	59
5:19–20	59

1 Peter

1:23	137
5:1–3	82
5:5	103, 153
5:8	51

2 Peter

1:3–4	40–41
2:1–3	87
3:16	87, 148

1 John

2:18	87
4:7–12	39
4:19	38

Revelation

Book of	131, 134, 151
5:10	133
22:15	94

✣ desiringGod

If you would like to further explore the vision of God and life presented in this book, we at Desiring God would love to serve you. We have hundreds of resources to help you grow in your passion for Jesus Christ and help you spread that passion to others. At our website, desiringGod.org, you'll find almost everything John Piper has written and preached, including more than thirty books. We've made over twenty-five years of his sermons available free online for you to read, listen to, download, and in some cases watch.

In addition, you can access hundreds of articles, listen to our daily internet radio program, find out where John Piper is speaking, learn about our conferences, discover our God-centered children's curricula, and browse our online store. John Piper receives no royalties from the books he writes and no compensation from Desiring God. The funds are all reinvested into our gospel-spreading efforts. DG also has a whatever-you-can-afford policy, designed for individuals with limited discretionary funds. If you'd like more information about this policy, please contact us at the address or phone number below. We exist to help you treasure Jesus Christ and his gospel above all things because he is most glorified in you when you are most satisfied in him. Let us know how we can serve you!

Desiring God
Post Office Box 2901
Minneapolis, Minnesota 55402

888.346.4700
mail@desiringGod.org
www.desiringGod.org